The Ideal Blend

W.T. Cockman

ISBN 0-9643285-0-X

Introduction

W hen we come to understand more fully, to appreciate more deeply, and to apply more diligently the basic tenets of the Christian faith, we are moving in the direction of an ideal blend that helps us achieve a balance in life. Our pilgrimage toward the goal of Christian maturity is more like a path than a straight line. The course a path takes is influenced by terrain and the objects in its way. So, it wanders through the woods or open spaces, sometimes straight ahead, but more often than not from side to side. Choices have to be made, not in relation to our ultimate goal, but as to how the rough terrain can be crossed or the objects can be passed. This book is designed to help us with those choices that we have to make almost daily in regard to which way our personal paths will go.

Each chapter is arranged so as to expand our understanding of the subject under consideration, to help us develop a deeper appreciation for it, and to get a grip on how to apply the truth to daily life. When these things happen the disparity between what we profess to be and who we actually are will be narrowed. The hunger of my life, for myself and others, is that we might attain the fullness of joy that comes when what we ought to be is who we are.

— W. T. Cockman

Contents

1

The Ideal Blend
Luke 10:33-35

One value of being a pastor in a small college town is that you can slip out of the office for a few minutes and watch the various athletic teams practice. I once stood alongside the basketball court with the coach as the team went through its various drills. "Coach," I asked, "What happens when a person gets his second wind?" He hesitated for a moment, as if in deep thought, and replied, "To put it in a layman's language, you get your second wind when all the different parts of the body synchronize to the faster pace."

Now, since I am a minister, that explanation by the coach set my mind to work about what relevance the word "synchronize" has to our Christian pilgrimage. It occurred to me that the word blend would sometimes be an adequate replacement for synchronize. Jesus used the word "wholeness" when He described the healthy state of existence to which He called us. He meant by wholeness, at least in part, that the various facets of our personalities had achieved a sense of oneness. That is, blending had occurred.

An urgent necessity we as Christians have is an ideal blend in thinking, feeling, and acting. A lack of balance in these areas stifles the goal of wholeness. The most poignant illustration of an ideal blend of thinking, feeling, and acting is contained in the parable of the Good Samaritan. The reaction of the Samaritan to the victim who had been robbed, beaten, and left for dead beside the road, affords us a prime example of the effectiveness of service to a person in need when an ideal blend of thinking, feeling, and acting is applied to a situation.

The Ideal Blend—An Example

Luke 10:33-35 contains an excellent example of the mind (thinking), emotions (feeling), and action (acting) working together in a blend to achieve a worthy end. An innocent traveler had fallen victim to thieves who stripped him and left him half dead. He needed immediate

1

attention. The priest and Levite passed him by, but then came the Samaritan. The biblical account of what happened in that encounter between the Samaritan and the helpless victim is so revealing about how thinking, feeling, and acting are such necessary elements in effective service.

The scriptural account records that the Samaritan, arriving at the scene, saw him. That means he viewed the situation. He analyzed it (thinking). A man had been robbed, stripped, and wounded, and was in dire circumstances. The Samaritan caught all these aspects in one sweeping view. That involved the use of his mind.

Then, the scripture declares he had compassion on him. What the Samaritan saw engendered an emotional response (feeling). Thus the motivational factor was added to the situation.

Next came the action. The Samaritan went to him, bound up his wounds, applied the medicine, supplied the first-century rescue unit (the donkey), accompanied him to the hospital (the inn), stayed with him through the night, paid his bill, and took into account the possibility of a need for extended care ("whatsoever thou spendest more . . ."). What a glorious example of an ideal blend of thinking, feeling, and acting! The mind not only analyzed the needs correctly but gave guidance to the action so that helpful deeds were done. The feeling of compassion impelled the Samaritan into action with correct motivation. The outcome was that a man who had fallen victim to robbers was rescued by a nameless Samaritan whose quality of life allowed him to think, to feel, and to act out the ideal blend.

The Ideal Blend—Out of "Sync"

One of my first jobs after marriage was working in the dyeing department at a hosiery mill. The formula for mixing exactly the right amount of dye for the desired color had to be followed with extreme exactness. The slightest variation from the formula could have unfavorable results. It is the same with the blend of thinking, feeling, and acting. When one of these is neglected in the formula, the outcome will be less than desired.

First, suppose we think and feel without acting. Then we begin to relish a religious setting that stimulates us mentally or emotionally but is devoid of application to daily life. We may walk around with our head in the sky or go all out emotionally. We choose those places where we are challenged to think or where an emotional feast is set before us. The visions that call for action are discarded as quickly as we would lay

2

aside an unwanted garment. Good intentions take the place of effective action. We know we "ought to" becomes a daily diet in our language. The "carry through" is missing. The Samaritan thought and felt—but also acted.

Second, we may think and act without feeling; therefore the motivational factor is missing. The "what" takes precedence over the "why." The way the action is carried out may be austere and cold, and the dignity of the individual may be ignored.

When I was a child, the mother from one of the poor families in our community would visit our home every three or four weeks. She would bring with her a sack, neatly rolled and tied with strings. As she came around the house she would throw the sack in the chimney corner. We children were under orders from our parents not to disturb the sack. We could look at it but were not to move it. Later in the visit, when the mother would prepare to leave, my stepmother would say, "Mary, let me give you some food"—to which Mary would answer, "Let me go get my sack."

Later in life I began to think on Mary's visits and wondered why she would throw her sack into the chimney corner instead of walking up to the house with it. It suddenly dawned on me. It was a matter of dignity. If she had come to the door with her sack in hand, she would have been asking for a handout. But, in her own simplicity of thinking, after my stepmother volunteered to give food, she felt it was OK to pick up her sack. Somehow her dignity remained intact.

The "why" and "how" we render a service is so important to the perfect blend. The act is enhanced enormously when the motivational force is love. The Samaritan felt compassion, and so his deeds were rendered with tenderness and understanding.

Third, we may feel and act without thinking. It is important, not that we do something, but that we do what is needful. So the mind must be involved to give direction to the feeling and acting. Mere activity may be as devoid of purpose as a bull in a china shop. What we feel and do should never circumvent the mind.

Note closely that every action by the Samaritan had purpose and design. The first aid, the ride to the inn, the personal care, the financial assistance—each was needful and in order. The feeling and acting accomplished something because the thinking was allowed to play its guiding role.

3

The Ideal Blend—Adjusting to the Need

The ideal blend in thinking, feeling, and acting does not mean that in every situation we emphasize each element to the same degree. There are those circumstances in which one of the three is to be dominant in order to accomplish a worthy goal. The other two will be present but to a lesser degree.

There are those situations when the thinking must come to the forefront. For example, a number of years ago, my family was attending a Sunday School class social. Our daughter, then a teenager, was playing hide-and-seek with another teenager. They both were racing to reach home base first. In their haste the teenage boy failed to spot a clothesline across the carport. It caught him under the chin, turning him upside down. His head literally bounced as it hit the cement floor. Immediately he was out of it.

Standing nearby I raced to his side. His face was turning blue, and he was gasping for air. The mother of the boy became hysterical. "Why doesn't someone do something?" she cried. I knew I was that someone. I called for help to put him into a station wagon to transport him to the emergency room at the nearest hospital. I rode beside him, giving assistance en route. Shortly after we arrived at the hospital and emergency service was rendered, he was, from all outward appearances, as good as new. Only then did my emotions—the feelings—rise up. The crisis over, it was OK to let the feelings come to the forefront. But, had this happened earlier, it could have impaired the necessary action.

There are other occasions when the feeling element needs to be dominant—a death has occurred, a teenager has run away from home, a new baby has arrived. These are the times when we need to feel with the family. Giving a theological discourse on the Christian view of death or a lecture on parent-child relationships at such a time would be totally out of order.

Then there are those times when action is the call of the hour. That was true with the Good Samaritan. Emotional expression of support alone would not have met the need; analyzing what had happened by itself would have been insufficient. A wounded man needed immediate help, and that called for action. So, most of the story focuses on the Samaritan's response in action.

Almost every situation in life calls for a variation in blend in order to have the ideal blend. Thinking, feeling, and acting need to be emphasized in accord with that which is most needed in responding to the occasion.

The Ideal Blend—Maintaining Our Uniqueness

We as individuals are different. Some of us are weighed more heavily in one of the three—thinking, feeling, or acting—than in the other two. Almost any variation can be found among us. How then does the word "blend" apply here?

Uniqueness is a special gift from God. Variety is the spice of life. How bland the world would be if everyone were the same in personality traits. Therefore, individuality must not be surrendered in search of a blend that would violate basic personality. God didn't make us like we are so we could smooth off all the rough corners and become like everyone else.

God's kingdom calls for the thinkers, the feelers, and the actors. To sit at the feet of the thinkers, and to explore depths of understanding hitherto hidden, is truly a privilege. To observe those persons whose capacity to feel has been developed until they identify with another's hurt or joy almost instantaneously, causes us to appreciate our differences. To see those individuals, whose insight leads them to spontaneously do what is needful in light of the occasion, makes us aware that variation of talents is truly a blessing.

However, when we are weighed in one direction—thinking, feeling, acting—to such an extent that our effectiveness is lessened, perhaps we should cultivate the other two a bit more in order to find a better blend. The person who walks around with his head in the clouds might get his hands dirty for a change. The individual whose emotions tend to run rampant might inject the guidance of his mind a little more into the picture. The one who views idleness as a curse, and must always be doing something regardless of its value, might ask the questions, "Where am I going?" "Why?" Even though we are different—thank God for that—it does not rule out the possibility of cultivating a better blend in order to be more useful. This we can do without violating our uniqueness.

One of the challenges for coaches, irrespective of the sport, is to help an athlete recognize his strengths and weaknesses, and then to help that athlete to hone his strengths and to upgrade those areas where weaknesses exist. This is done without crushing the athlete's uniqueness, his basic personality. One has only to watch a team perform to recognize the variation in personalities which make up the team. One player may go about the task at hand in a methodical, contemplative fashion. Another may openly show his feelings and may perform basically on a wave of emotion. Another player just gets to the job done.

His role is not that of the acute thinking or the deep feeling. But day in and day out he comes to play.

So it is with the Christian life. Each of us is unique. We have various roles to play. No one is greater than someone else, merely different. Each person is pivotal in forming the team.

The Ideal Blend—and the States of Life

Life is change; change means adjustments. One basic fact we have learned about adulthood more than ever is: it is not static. Circumstances beyond our control pound at life and demand some sort of adjustment. Even those matters over which we do have some control usher in certain changes to life. The perfect blend of thinking, feeling, and acting also is affected by life's transitional stages. The perfect blend is not a patterned response meticulously designed for every stage of life. The young adult may coach the softball team (acting). Later in life he may find that physiological changes may mean that he attends the game to watch his son play (feeling). He may encourage his son and share with him certain nuances of the game that will improve his play (thinking).

When my father reached the age of his late seventies and early eighties he found it necessary to depend on me in the decision-making process (thinking). He said to me one day, "Pid" (my nickname which only my father used), "the time may come when you will need to make some decisions for me. I want you to take over and do just that should the occasion arise" (acting). This meant that my father and I would switch roles in the future. When I was a child he made most of the decisions. I depended on him; now he was going to depend on me.

One day when I was visiting my father he made another request. "Pid," he asked, "I want you to preach my funeral." The emotional level shot up rather quickly (feeling). My first reaction was, *No, I can't do it* (feeling). Then my better judgment began to take over (thinking). I said, "Pap, I'll try" (acting). Nothing in my past experiences had prepared me for this type of occasion. Other stages of life had made their particular demands. Now I was having to face another stage when a parent was aware he would soon die. To fulfill my responsible role at this stage of life, it was necessary to seek a workable blend in thinking, feeling, and acting, which would allow me to respond to my father's request in the most meaningful way.

The Ideal Blend—and Our Approaches to God

John A. Redhead, a prominent Presbyterian minister, authored a book entitled *Getting to Know God.*[1] The book has a chapter entitled "Pathways to God." The thesis of the chapter is that in our approaches to God we move along those pathways in keeping with whether we are primarily thinkers, feelers, or actors. For example, the person who responds to God chiefly through thinking will not be the one who shouts "amen" loudly in the worship service. He is not devoid of feeling but is acting in accord with his nature when the thinking (mind) plays the primary role in his worship.

On the other hand the person who responds to God primarily through his feelings (emotions) will be perfectly at home in a worship service where heartwarming experiences are shared. Warmth is extremely important in interpersonal relationships to this individual. He is open in his expression of feelings.

The third approach to God is for the practical person. He expresses his devotion to God chiefly through action (acting). Again, he is not devoid of thinking and feeling. It merely happens that his pathway to God falls mainly in the line of doing.

Now, what value do the preceding insights have in relation to the perfect blend? It would seem that the first value is that we can recognize the fact that people respond to God differently. To do so will lead to greater understanding and better relationships in the Christian community.

Second, we can avoid the "everybody-ought-to-be-like-me" syndrome. Birds of a feather do flock together, even in the Christian faith. We tend to gather around us people somewhat like ourselves and to exclude those who are different. Churches, and even denominations, spring up in accord with a given group's patterned response to God.

I once served in a large city where there were many Baptist churches. Each church, it seemed, had a given personality. Those people whose pathway to God corresponded with a church's personality tended to go to that church.

Third, we can learn to appreciate people whose responses to God are different from ours. To be different from us is not to be less than us. God needs those who love Him chiefly with the mind, or the heart, or through action.

The Ideal Blend — As Apprehension, Appreciation, and Application

Wholesome Christian growth includes three elements: Apprehension (thinking), Appreciation (feeling), and Application (acting). The growth process is set in motion as a person gains additional information or new insights relative to some area where a need is being felt. The additional information or new insights are grasped by and assimilated into the mind (apprehension). As one expands his understanding, there is developed a positive feeling concerning what is being learned (appreciation). A certain attitudinal tone is developed. Having come to an expanded understanding of and a deeper appreciation for a given truth, one decides to act on the basis of the additional information or new insight (application). So the process of Christian growth has reached full cycle.

Let's look at an example of this process in action as it relates to a given subject area, namely forgiveness. Forgiveness is often mistakenly viewed as an instantaneous act rather than a process. This has come about because what we see openly is the act of forgiveness and not what preceded the act or what comes after the act. But for forgiveness to reach its full meaning for us, we need to go through the steps of apprehension, appreciation, and application.

First, we need to think through what forgiveness really is (apprehension). Some common definitions are quite inadequate. How many times have we heard the words "forgive and forget"? To eradicate from the mind what has been stored there, i.e., to forget, is not possible. So forgiveness must be something other than forgetting.

Or, consider the flippant view that forgiveness is an easy matter that one can issue almost at will. An area such as forgiveness, however, which always has an emotional base, requires time, because emotional adjustment is a process. The emotions cannot be hurried, and, if we try to do so, superficiality will be the result. Even after forgiveness has been extended, the emotional adjustment and practical application continue.

A better definition of forgiveness perhaps is one that follows: "Forgiveness is not so much to forget as it is not to allow a wrong to destroy a relationship." With such a definition, it seems to me, we are getting somewhere. To forgive is to take a wrong and to deal with it in such a fashion that a relationship remains intact, though disturbed momentarily. The goal, therefore, in forgiveness is not to forget, but to work through the tension created by the wrong in such a way that the relationship can be re-established. And, even when the relationship cannot be resumed as before, to develop a positive attitude toward the "What is" so negativism is not allowed to permeate the situation.

When forgiveness is understood as defined above, a positive feeling is developed toward it, because one is no longer frustrated by an impractical and faulty understanding. Appreciation grows with expanded knowledge. One of the tragedies of life is that we call for closure on an idea or concept long before it has had time to grow and expand. As a result the appreciation level remains lower than it should.

Accompanying greater understanding and deeper appreciation is the desire to make practical application of a given truth. When we begin to practice forgiveness, we learn its practical value. Life seems to work better when we forgive rather than when we hold grudges. The result is that our discovery that forgiveness works in life stimulates a desire for greater understanding and creates a deeper appreciation. Therefore, application enhances apprehension and appreciation. So the process goes on, no longer in a one-, two-, three-step cycle, but all intermingled with each element—thinking, feeling, and acting—stimulating the other two so the growth cycle becomes an adventure. An ideal blend of apprehension, appreciation, and application is occurring.

The Ideal Blend—As Others See Us

Being evaluated by others can be a scary experience, but one that is most valuable. How we see ourselves may be very similar to how others see us. But, on the other hand, it may be vastly different. The subjective element is present in all of us. To be evaluated by others is one way of narrowing the gap between how we see ourselves and how others see us.

Now, how does evaluation by others relate to the ideal blend? It relates in this manner. More often than not, other people "size us up" as thinkers, feelers, or actors. The statement, "That man really has a head on his shoulders," means that a person has been classified as a thinker. "You know, she really cares about people. She is one of the best listeners I know." Those statements indicate that one has been identified as a feeler. "If you want someone to do something for you, just ask Jim." So, Jim has been picked as a doer. Again let me say, to be identified as a thinker, or feeler, or actor, does not mean that the other two elements are missing. It does mean that perhaps we are slanted more in one direction than in the other two. Where we fit does not have a good or bad connotation. It is simply a recognition of our strength either as a thinker, feeler, or actor.

At the time of this writing, I am preparing to lead a single-adult retreat. One of the activities in which we will engage is an evaluation of how we are seen by others. Personal relationships can be enhanced immensely when we are permitted through group activity to step outside ourselves and look in on ourselves through the eyes of others. Not only

9

can personal relationships be strengthened through this procedure, but we can arrive at a more workable blend of thinking, feeling, and acting.

Sometime, unbeknown to us, we are slanted so heavily in the direction of thinking or feeling or acting that our emphasis on that aspect of our personality, and our neglect of the other two, may lead to strained relationships or ineffective service. One way of correcting this imbalance is through becoming aware of how we are viewed by others. Their insight as to whether or not we are out of kilter can be invaluable.

Recently I was asked to give my insight as to how a relationship could be strengthened between a husband and wife. It was quite obvious that the husband was the thinker, and the wife was the feeler. The husband's approach to the decision-making process was to think it through. The head played the greatest part. It was not that he did not feel deeply, or that he failed to act. He simply needed to weigh matters.

The wife, on the other hand, undertook any issue primarily through the gate of feeling. Emotion played the greatest part. Logic was secondary to the heart. To give valid reasons (thinking) as to why a given action ought to be taken would not be convincing to the wife. She just did not arrive at decisions like that.

My task, therefore, was not to induce the thinker to stop thinking or the feeler to stop feeling, but to help them see how they differed. When the thinker saw that he was a thinker, and the feeler saw that she was a feeler, a basis for understanding occurred. Then the thinker could appreciate his wife's approach to issues as a feeler, and the wife could appreciate her husband's approach to issues as a thinker. A better blend had been created. Out of this better blend should come more productive and meaningful action.

The Ideal Blend—The Conclusion

The purpose for this chapter has not been to portray one personality type as superior to another, but to make us aware of how we differ. Through this heightened awareness it is hoped that appreciation for one another, even with our differences, will be elevated. One of my favorite songs has a line which goes, "It takes us all to feed the hungry crowd." Each one of us is needed in God's economy. We need the thinkers to think, the feelers to feel, and the actors to act. When all of God's people with their varying talents link hand in hand with one common goal— service to our Master—we will have arrived at a proper blend.

1. John A. Redhead, *Getting To Know God* (New York: Abingdon Press, 1954), 37-44.

2

Our Awareness Levels

One spring, right before Easter, the Pine Valley Baptist Church in Wilmington, North Carolina, asked me to lead a retreat for their single adults, using as a biblical base the seven sayings of Jesus on the cross. The necessary preparation was made, and the retreat was completed. Upon returning home, my mind continued to explore the depth of meaning contained in Jesus' sayings.

New insight came which had eluded me earlier. That new insight was that each of Jesus' statements on the cross contained an awareness level on which He was operating, even under those dire circumstances. He was intensely aware of the needs of the people around the cross, His own desire for unbroken relationship with His Father, and the cry of His body for release from the pain. So, let us view each one of Christ's statements independently and examine the awareness level which each saying indicates.

The Why Awareness Level

"Father, forgive them; for they know not what they do" (Luke 23:34).

Seeking to understand why a given act is committed is characteristic of the forgiving heart. Jesus looked underneath the ghastly deed of the cross and tried to understand why it was done — "they know not what they do." If the people had really understood the horror of the act, they would have turned and fled the mocking scene. The senseless howls of the mob and the cruel jibes of the "churchmen" were understood by Jesus as being based on ignorance.

The forgiving heart thinks that way. Undeserved blows rendered would have become strokes of love had understanding been complete. Ignorance does not justify a wrong act, but making an attempt to understand the motivation underlying the deed is to live on a higher awareness level than to accept everything at face value.

It does not surprise me that the first words uttered by Jesus on the cross were a prayer for forgiveness. He was practicing, amid excruciating pain, what He had taught and lived in the world. He was living in accord with a Why awareness level which was a part of His life-style.

I understand the Why is a level of awareness that tends to open the gates of forgiveness. The why of the wrong, while not excusing the wrong or accepting it as final, may help us to forgive the wrong.

On January 9, 1984, an issue of *Time* magazine carried an article entitled "I Spoke . . . as a Brother."[1] The subhead read: "A pardon from the pontiff, a lesson in forgiveness for a troubled world." The article described the extraordinary scene of Pope John II huddled in intense conversation with his would-be assassin, Mehmet Ali Agca. A photographer had accompanied the Pope to the cell where Agca was held because the Pope wanted the image in that cell to be shown around a world filled with nuclear arsenals and unforgiving hatreds. John Paul's words were intended for Agca alone. "What we talked about will have to remain a secret between him and me," the Pope reported as he emerged from the cell. "I spoke to him as a brother, whom I have pardoned, and who has my complete trust."

While not trying to read into the Pope's action something that may not have been there, it would seem that the Why awareness level was present. He must have made some effort to understand the background from which Agca came and how those factors contributed to the attack upon his life. Forgiving people invariably take into account the Why of a given act. So, Jesus' first saying on that cross indicates a Why awareness level.

The Needs Awareness Level

"Today shalt thou be with me in paradise" (Luke 23:43).

The first words of Jesus on the cross were a prayer. The second words were in answer to a prayer. A request was made expressing a need, and Jesus responded to that need. Even when His own need was so immense, He was sensitive to the need of another. Contrast Jesus' response with our own tendency to become caught up in our own needs so we are unable to hear or see the needs of others. Jesus responded to the request of the thief because He was attuned to the cry of others. He was aware of Needs.

Jesus' response, in this case, was in behalf of a single individual. Those who have developed the Needs awareness level don't merely see masses of people but individuals within the masses. They don't simply hear the roar of the crowd, but the single voices within the crowd.

The number of occasions when Jesus gave prime time to one person during His earthly ministry continues to amaze me. He spoke to the Samaritan woman at Jacob's well about living water which, when you drink it, you will never thirst again. Amidst the pressing throng He became aware of the touch of faith by the woman with the issue of blood. He took the time to visit for a meal in the home of Zacchaeus. Only the person who is aware of needs will give attention to single individuals. But it is through responding to single requests that we keep alive our sensitivity to the masses.

The thief's request was a simple one—"Remember me." Jesus' promise that on that very day the thief would join Him in paradise must have been comforting indeed, for our severest pain is not physical but relational. Nothing hurts quite so much as to be isolated in aloneness, especially the aloneness of death. Jesus rose above His own pain to help another in pain to promise him companionship in death.

As a special worker with adults in Sunday School, one of my tasks is to help groups to remain open to newcomers. Unless classes take definite, planned actions to remain open, they tend to become closed to outsiders. One acid test of whether a group is open or closed is discovered by what group members do when they first enter the department or class. Those groups that are open have members who look first for the visitor, rather than for the familiar face. Open groups gravitate toward persons who need their attention. They think first of the needs of others and, in doing so, discover their own cups filled with God's marvelous grace. To develop a Needs awareness level transforms our own lives into more meaningful avenues of service.

The Responsibility Awareness Level

"Woman, behold thy son! Behold thy Mother!" (John 19:26-27).

Early in His ministry Jesus expressed a Responsibility awareness level. "The Spirit of the Lord is upon me, because he hath anointed me to preach to the poor; he hath sent me to heal the brokenhearted, to preach deliverance to the captives, and recovering of sight to the blind, to set at liberty them that are bruised, to preach the acceptable year of the Lord" (Luke 4:18-19). Here at the end of His earthly ministry, He took on the responsibility of caring for His mother by committing her care to John. That He would see His mother standing nearby while hanging on the cross indicates an awareness level that can be understood only in the light of His incomparable love for His mother.

Again note that Jesus didn't see just a crowd but two individuals within the crowd, His mother and John. He saw His mother in the light of her hurt and future need. Since He was the oldest son, the Responsibility awareness level stepped in. She needed a home. Home is more than a place to live; it is a place to love. John was the right one to provide His mother that type of security.

Jesus saw another face within the milling crowd. It belonged to John, the beloved disciple. John seemed to have a knack for being near Jesus; and when one is near, he can be helpful. So, Christ entrusted His mother to him. This beloved friend was near in person because he was near in love. John was willing to enter the danger zone, that of shame and suffering; as a result, he entered the zone of usefulness as well. He was permitted to do for Jesus what Jesus could not do for Himself.

My mother died when I was five years old. I was the baby of eleven children. All the children were still at home at the time of my mother's death. One of the last acts by my mother was to extend her arm and pull me close to her. To recall that incident, as you might suppose, stirs certain emotions within my heart. Often I have wondered how my mother felt at that moment. Knowing that she was dying, there had to be a keen sense of responsibility on her part. Who would take care of her children? Especially, who would take care of her baby boy? My father also must have felt a tremendous weight on his shoulders.

There comes a times with all of us when the cloak of responsibility must be passed to another. There must be considerable consolation in knowing that awaiting the passing of the mantel are loving, faithful disciples who form another link in the chain of God's eternal work. Such a disciple was John. His prompt obedience to Jesus' request indicated a ready willingness. Love does not long ponder the needed action.

The Relational Awareness Level

"My God, my God, why hast thou forsaken me?" (Matthew 27:46).

To feel deserted at any time is tragic enough. To feel deserted while on a cross must be unbearable.

Jesus was so aware of relationships, especially His relationship with His Father, that the slightest breach in that closeness brought a cry of anguish from His lips. Jesus had declared earlier to His disciples, "Behold the time cometh, yea, is now come, that ye shall be scattered,

14

every man to his own, and shall leave me alone: and yet I am not alone, because the Father is with me" (John 16:32). But now the Father's face was hidden. The macabre aspects of the cross rested their climax not just in the physical pain, but in the dread of being forsaken.

This feeling of aloneness was so hard for Jesus to bear because it was so in contrast to what He had known. "I and my Father are one" (John 10:30), He had emphasized. "I am in the Father, and the Father in me" (John 14:14). How could there be a closer relationship? Feeling deserted, then, was a new experience in the life of Jesus.

The closer the relationship, the more hurtful the pain when that relationship is disturbed. The person who walks from a lighted room into darkness becomes keenly aware of the darkness. So strong had been Jesus' relationship with the Father that any interruption was unbearably horrifying.

People who experience deep relationships are those who are in contact with their feelings. To verbalize those feelings adds to the depth of a relationship, especially when the feelings are shared without blame. Here Jesus not only identifies His feeling but shares that feeling with His Father. As a result, He was able to move through His darkest hour into the dawn of a new day — "Father, into thy hands I commend my Spirit" (Luke 23:46).

All of us need to learn that it is OK to feel lonely. Interrupted, even broken, relationships are a part of life. The result of such severance is pain. To admit that we are hurting is a part of healing. To accept our pain and to go into it is eventually to go through it. When we stop and hurt, one day at a time, we allow the healing process to occur. Then there comes that time when we can let go of the pain.

A church member who had lost his wife through death once shared with me that moment when the healing process had culminated. "I turned off onto the street on which our house was located," he confessed. "It was night and as the car lights flashed down the street, I knew it was time to close the pages on that part of my life. It was time to move on."

Another man, working through a divorce, approached me in the church yard after I had delivered a sermon on the topic, "It's OK to Be Lonely." He was in the beginning phase of grief—admitting it. He said, "I just wanted you to know that I'm hurting, but you helped me a great deal by letting me know that it's OK to hurt."

God's Son hurt, too. He was so aware of relationships that the feeling of being forsaken was the sorest of pain.

15

The Physical Awareness Level

"I thirst" (John 19:28).

It is interesting to note that Jesus didn't say, "My hands hurt or My feet hurt," but rather, "I thirst." The wounded body often develops an unquenchable thirst. Jesus became aware of this physical need to replenish the body. He was thirsty.

One of my first chores on the farm was to carry fresh, cool water from the well to the fields where my father and other members of the family were working. My father was a tireless worker and perspired freely. He would be so thirsty that when it came his turn to drink from the common jar, he couldn't drink fast enough. Often water would trickle down his chin onto his shirt. Remembering this experience from my childhood serves as a reminder to me of what it is to be awfully thirsty.

Jesus' request for water came after much of the ordeal of the cross was behind Him (John 19:28). So, it was at the beginning of His ministry when He had fasted forty days and forty nights — "He was afterward an hungered" (Matthew 4:2). An athlete in the course of an exciting game forgets his injury. Only after the game is over does the real pain attract his attention.

Christ's awareness of His physical need indicates again His humanity. Not only was He divine, but human as well. He faced life as we face it. Pain was real to Him. He was thirsty as you and I are thirsty. It means a lot to me to realize that when I help someone who is thirsty to have a drink of water, I am responding to Christ's words, "I am thirsty." He taught us that when we help someone else, in a true sense we are helping Him. I was not there by the cross to respond to His thirst, but I can now respond to the thirst of people around me, and know that in doing so I am responding to Christ.

The Task Awareness Level

"It is finished" (John 19:30).

The Task awareness level was one on which Jesus operated throughout His life. "For I came down from heaven, not to do mine own will, but the will of him that sent me" (John 6:38). Again Christ said, "I have glorified thee on the earth: I have finished the work which thou gavest me to do" (John 17:4). Christ was on an assignment, a mission for His Father.

It was not an easy task. "O my Father, if it be possible, let this cup pass from me: nevertheless not as I will, but as thou wilt" (Matthew 26:39). God doesn't promise us rose gardens. He does ask us to be true to our assignment in spite of the difficulty involved. No task of ours will ever supersede the demands of Christ's task. Yet, He was true to His assignment. We can be true to ours.

The joy of a completed task moderates the pain (see Hebrews 12:2). High purpose leads to steadfast endurance. To know that one's task has as its end a worthy goal gives meaning to the sacrificial demands of the moment. Jesus stated His dream—to do God's will—and lived out of His dream.

The greater the demands of a task, the greater the feeling of accomplishment. The words, "It is finished," are only one word in the original language. I wonder what tone of voice Jesus used when He spoke the word. My personal feeling is that it had the sound of triumph.

Through completing His task, Jesus made possible the redemption of the world — "Greater love hath no man than this, that a man lay down his life for his friends" (John 15:13).

The Trust Awareness Level

"Father, into thy hands I commend my spirit" (Luke 23:36).

The commitment of His spirit to the Father showed that Jesus had moved through His earlier feeling of desertion to the level of trust. The accomplishment of the Trust level is always a process. It doesn't come by simply pushing a button labeled "trust." It comes as a result of living through the "hard knocks" of life with undiminished devotion. We can't always see the end of the tunnel at the entrance gate. But to believe that there is light at the end of the tunnel, even while in the midst of darkness, is to move toward the level of undaunted trust.

Jesus' commitment statement is found in Psalms 31:5. To the statement discovered in Psalms 31, Jesus adds the word Father. He was going home to One He knew well.

Generally speaking we die as we live. Trust is not a feeling we can conjure up just for the emergency. It must be hammered out on the anvil of daily faithfulness.

Funeral sermons require tremendous preparation. I usually pick a theme prevalent in the life of the deceased and expand on it. One such funeral message carried the title "It's Time to Go Now." The man was ill for some time in the hospital. He became increasingly aware that the

17

end of life was near. He would say to his wife, "It's time to go now." Perhaps he had used these words other times in life's many departures. He used them again in the final departure as he anticipated crossing the gulf of death.

It is so fitting that the last statement of Jesus on the cross was one of trust. His Father had not left Him alone. The Father's arms were extended to receive His Son back into the heavens from which He had departed for awhile in order to accomplish the mission of redemption for the world.

Awareness as a Life-style

At a board of ministers meeting at Campbell University, Winston and Winnie Pearce really caught my attention. They sat on the opposite side of the table. My admiration for them as a loving couple grew upon observing the common courtesies they showed toward each other. Winston was the perfect gentleman as he seated Winnie. Winnie was the perfect listener when Winston talked. Their facial expressions indicated they were very aware of each other. Why shouldn't it be that way in all relationships?

The church ought to be the one place where we are intensely aware of one another. The church is a body. If one member suffers, we all suffer. When one member rejoices, we all rejoice. The goal of redemption moves beyond the forgiveness of our sins. God wants to recreate us (2 Corinthians 5:17). To be made new is to be lifted to a higher awareness level.

Our pastor, David Hull,* was serving a newly established church in Charlotte, North Carolina, at the same time I was adult minister at the First Baptist Church there. One day when I was leaving the associational office, David and two other ministers were chatting in the parking lot. As I walked by, David turned and acknowledged me with a gesture of the hand. It was a simple thing to do and yet so revealing. David was acting in accord with an awareness level which had developed into a life-style. Now, serving on the same staff with him, it doesn't seem out of place at all when David comes by my office and asks, "Anything you need?" He is merely being himself.

Christ on the cross depicted awareness levels which sprang from a life-style. He was living out under the cruelest of circumstances what He had honed in the crucible of daily life. The cross was not a place where superficial acts were in order. One's true nature comes out under those circumstances.

18

The levels of awareness on which we operate can be intensified. There is no better way for this to happen than to develop a closer relationship with Him who was ever aware of the circumstances around Him.

1. "I Spoke As a Brother," *Time*, January 9, 1984, 27-33.

* David Hull now serves as pastor of the First Baptist Church, Knoxville, Tennessee.

3

Take with You Words

Serendipitous experiences come to us unannounced. Such was the case when I was asked to write the teaching procedures for the 1990 Adult Vacation Bible School material. The main Bible study was on the books of Amos and Hosea. Even though the Minor Prophets had received special attention in my personal Bible study, my preparation for the writing assignment opened up new discoveries beyond measure. One of those discoveries is the subject of this chapter.

Hosea, like many of the prophets, was calling the people back to God. But his instruction to the people relative to the manner of that return is unique. Listen to him: "O Israel, return unto the Lord thy God; for thou hast fallen by thine iniquity. Take with you words, and turn to the Lord: say unto him, Take away all iniquity, and receive us graciously: so will we render the calves of our lips" (Hosea 14:1-2).

Note the instruction concerning the manner of their return to God: Take with you words. Why words? Surely some tangible gift would be more appropriate. But would it be? The psalmist learned that gifts are not always what God desires: "For thou desirest not sacrifice; else would I give it: thou delightest not in burnt offerings. The sacrifices of God are a broken spirit: a broken and contrite heart, O God, thou wilt not despise" (Psalm 51:16-17).

When relationships are disturbed—as was the case between Israel and God—one of the most difficult approaches is to return with words. It is much easier to present a gift than to admit "I was wrong" or "I have sinned." To verbalize our true feelings is not at all easy. Words have a way of revealing what is inside of us so we no longer can hide behind perfunctory deeds.

When relationships are awry, then why do we hesitate so long in turning to words? Why do we try to make substitutes when words are what are most needed? Might it be that talking out the troubled area is not a frequent practice with us? Do we think it better to stew in silence?

Or do we find it difficult to express our feelings? Or is it because words have a way of revealing the attitudes underlying the deed?

Intensified religious activity does not always indicate deeper relationships. In fact, it can be a coverup for a relationship gone bad. Somehow we have mistakenly given the idea that the depth of relationships and the number of deeds performed are closely correlated, irrespective of the motivation involved. So, amount, not quality, becomes the measuring stick.

Healthy relationships are expressed in deeds, but not deeds devoid of right attitudes. Why a given act is rendered determines to a great extent the value of the act. When deeds performed are lacking in feeling, relationships have an empty ring. Very often deeds continue, at least for awhile, when relationships have gone sour. That's why we need words, for words add feeling to our deeds. To be sure, even words can be used superficially, but without words our relationships are missing a necessary dimension.

Hosea's admonition that the people return to God taking words with them has an interesting parallel in the New Testament that assumes the form of an example. When the Prodigal Son returned to his father, he took with him words (Luke 15:18-19). The words were descriptive of his state of being. They were well-chosen words, designed as a speech, and were to be delivered to his father when he reached home. The Prodigal Son understood that in the restoration of a relationship, words are essential.

"Why are words so important to relationships?" you may ask. "What do words do which make them so important?" Taking the Prodigal's speech as a backdrop to Hosea's counseling his people to return to God with words, let us see if we can answer the above questions.

Words Express Inner Feelings

"To tell you my THOUGHTS is to locate myself in a category. To tell you about my FEELINGS is to tell you about me." [1] Through words we may express our feelings. Words allow us to ventilate our feelings, to tell someone else what is inside. It is important to relationships that we express what we are feeling, both for our benefit and for the benefit of the other party involved. Many a troubled area has been settled peaceably when feelings became known. We cannot expect others to guess correctly what we are feeling. We need to express our feelings with words.

When the Prodigal Son returned to his father with his prepared speech, he expressed what he was feeling: "I am unworthy." Unworthy is a feeling word. The Prodigal's sense of self-worth had been shot; self-esteem had vanished. He had left home with a glint in his eye anticipating what awaited him barely over the hill. He was returning home beaten in spirit.

When feelings are expressed, it allows for intelligent, meaningful response to those feelings. The father's reaction to the Prodigal's sense of unworthiness was to do those things that indicated his undiminished love for his lost son. He did those things which would rebuild his son's feeling of self-worth. He embraced him; he had the servants bring a robe to replace his tattered one; a ring was put on his finger and shoes on his feet. A banquet was prepared of the best food possible—a grain-fed calf. Music was arranged so the occasion could be celebrated with dancing, an expression of merriment. Every act of acceptance of the son by his father bolstered the Prodigal's feeling of self-worth. The father was able to respond to his son's homecoming with the appropriate actions because his son had expressed to him in words what he was feeling.

All of us have needs. To make those needs known deepens relationships. Expressing what we are feeling is a main means of making our needs known. Silence is not a virtue if it means suppressing our feelings, for words are the channel through which we express our inner feelings.

It is essential to remember that God is not shocked when we express our feelings to Him. He knows them already. We need to entrust inner emotions with God so He can help us handle those feelings positively. Let us return to God with words.

Words Reveal Desire

Words are like windows to the soul which allow us and others to look inside and see our deepest desires. These longings may be hidden until we express them in words. The Prodigal in his prepared speech expressed his desire to the father: "Make me as one of your hired servants." The Prodigal just wanted to be home regardless of position. He had left home of his own free will. Perhaps there was a bit of arrogance involved, but his experience in the far country had changed all that. Home was the place he desired to be.

To express a desire in words gives meaning to the desire. The father could probably have guessed what his lost son wanted when he saw him coming in the distance, but his son's expression of his desire added meaning to the occasion both for the father and the son. We hesitate too often in adding words to life's experiences, and we are the losers thereby.

One of my older sisters always closes our conversations over the phone by saying, "I love you." I want to repeat the "I love you," but sometimes find difficulty in doing so. It is not because I do not love deeply. It springs rather from a reticence born of my childhood. I grew up in a large family where love was not expressed in words. That background sometimes places fences around my intention to express my desires. I am working at it and am seeing some improvement, but childhood fences are hard to hurdle. Whenever I hesitate to express in words my desire to say, "I love you," there is a feeling of emptiness inside, for I know that experiences without words have a missing element.

As was stated earlier about feelings, we cannot expect other people to guess our desires. Openness and honesty are called for. Verbal expression of our desires is a must in the deepening of our relationships with God and others. Certainly it is understood that what is referred to here is more than a petty selfishness. It speaks rather of needs common to us all—the need to be loved, the need to employ our talents, the need to be needed, the need for some sense of security. We must find avenues to express these needs wholesomely and profoundly.

The Arabs have a beautiful description of friendship. A friend, they say, is one to whom one may pour out all the content of one's heart, chaff and grain together, knowing that the gentlest of hands will take and sift it, keep what is worth keeping, and with the breath of kindness blow the rest away.

The Wednesday evening teacher-training session served as a forum for a divorcé to share the pain through which he had gone in the separation and subsequent divorce from his wife. "I was experiencing all the emotions of a death," he confided, "but no one seemed to be aware. I was expected to continue to perform on my job as if nothing was happening. Had my wife died, these expectations would have been altered accordingly, but all around me were people who avoided talking with me about my divorce. I needed so much for someone to understand my pain."

Needs must be expressed in words, or else we run the risk of our longings being hidden. Choice should be made about when and where and to whom we share, but remaining silent should not be an option.

Words Uncap Suppressed Sin

Our lives have been compared to the sea, only in reverse. The sea, as has often been suggested, has all its unrest on the surface, where it churns and tosses. But as you explore the depth, you find unbroken calm. Human life seems to be the reverse of that. Our lives on the surface seem calm and unruffled, as though everything were under control. But underneath are tumult, unrest, disquiet. So it is with suppressed sin. The outward acts of religious observance may continue for a person as if nothing is wrong, but there is a churning inside. Religious performance, though faithfully followed, has become a routine from which all meaning is gone. Confession—the return to God with words—is an attempt to bring the tumult to the surface where it can be met and dealt with.

Suppressed sin, like suppressed steam, is hazardous. Confession is the safety valve. Acknowledging our sins to God is like taking a bottle, removing the cap, tilting it, and pouring out the content. Words uncap suppressed sin.

When the Prodigal returned home to the father he poured out his heart with words, "Father, I have sinned against heaven and before thee." Confession is a valid and indispensable experience in one's return to God. The griefs, the sorrows, the hidden grudges, the desire for revenge, the burden of remorse for some unconfessed sin—all must be brought to the surface and shared with God before healing can occur.

Confession to one another, as James advises, is a widespread practice in certain areas of our day. A college student who was an alcoholic once came to me, requesting a conference in which he was to confess all his past sins in detail. It was one requirement in his rehabilitation. Needless to note, the session was a long one accompanied by intense emotional pain on his part. Later I evaluated the session. As I did so, it occurred to me that the confession of each sin was a way of bringing it to the surface, tripping the release valve—uncapping it—so that healing could result.

The Prodigal Son, then, was right on target when he returned to his father with words, which included confession of his sin. The goal of confession is forgiveness. One wants to have the slate wiped clean. Deeds without words are not enough in this process. We are to confess our sins (1 John 1:9).

Words Heal Broken Relationships

To be estranged from someone for whom we care deeply elicits the most intense pain. Hosea experienced this brokenness in his own domestic relationship. His wife, Gomer, left home to play the harlot. She left behind Hosea and three children. Many think that Hosea's theology, his concept of God, was broadened by his tragic experience. He viewed unfaithfulness, the betrayal of trust, as the worst of sins. He also saw the unfailing love of God in His willingness to take back Israel if only she would repent. He exemplified this quality of love in buying back his own wife when he saw her up for sale as a slave (Hosea 3:2). So, when Hosea admonished Israel to return to God, taking with them words, it was for the purpose of healing a broken relationship: "I will heal their backsliding, I will love them freely: for mine anger is turned away from him" (Hosea 14:4).

The prodigal returned to the father with words, and out of the encounter came the healing of a broken relationship. "But when he was yet a far way off, his father saw him, and had compassion, and ran, and fell on his neck, and kissed him" (Luke 15:20). So many disturbed relationships could be healed if communication were present. "Talk it out" might well correspond to Hosea's counsel that Israel return to God with "words." Tension points find release valves in understanding brought about by improved communication.

While I was pastor at the First Baptist Church, Elon College, North Carolina, we had what we called Teen-College for our youth in Vacation Bible School. One year the parable of the Prodigal Son served as a basis for our Bible study. The youth group was given the assignment to write an imaginary ending to the story of the Prodigal Son. The assignment was to be done over a four-day period. In their imaginary ending, the youth saw the elder brother as continuing his animosity toward his younger brother. In fact, with the passing of the years his hatred intensified. The mother in the family suffered much because of the rift. She died without witnessing any attempt at reconciliation by her oldest son.

One day when the two sons were alone out in the fields, the elder brother attacked his younger brother. A severe blow was struck, and the younger brother was sorely wounded. The elder brother ran away. The servants discovered the younger son and carried him to the house.

Meanwhile, out in the woods and alone, the elder brother began to do some serious thinking. He recalled how he had caused so much pain to his family, especially to his mother. He began to realize how his

25

hatred had consumed him. It led him to tears. He fell on his knees in prayer. He remembered the reception of the younger brother when he returned home. Then and there he decided to return home, too.

When the father saw him coming, he ran out to greet him. He carried him to the room where the younger brother was being tended. The elder brother moved to the side of the bed. His eyes met the eyes of his younger brother, and he saw forgiveness there. The eyes of the younger brother then closed in death.

I have often wondered why the youth closed the story where they did. I wanted to know more. What happened later? But that's what imaginary stories do for you. Perhaps the most important fact was that a relationship had been healed.

Words Restore Lost Position

"For this my son was dead, and is alive again; he was lost, and is found" (Luke 15:24) are words from the father which speak of restoration. His lost son would not return as a hired servant; he would return as a son. Though conditions within the family would not be as they were before, so far as the elder brother was concerned (Luke 15:28), there was no hesitancy at restoration on the part of the father. The estrangement was not to be permanent.

Hosea described the restoration process in picturesque language in relation to Israel's return to God with words.

"I will be as the dew unto Israel: he shall grow as the lily, and cast forth his roots as Lebanon. I will heal their faithlessness; I will love them freely, for my anger has turned from them. I will be as the dew to Israel; he shall blossom as the lily, he shall strike root as the poplar; his roots shall spread out; his beauty shall be like the olive, and his fragrance like Lebanon. They shall return and dwell beneath my shadow, they shall flourish as a garden; they shall blossom as the vine, their fragrance shall be like the wine of Lebanon" (Hosea 14:5-7).

There are three words used in the New Testament to depict the restoration of fallen mankind to God the Creator. Each word carries a picture which envisions what happens in that restoration. To see the pictures is to understand what it is to be returned to the family of God.

The first word is "redemption." It pictures an enslaved man being set free. He has no claim whereby to earn his freedom, but God, out of His infinite grace, sets him free. He is no longer a slave, but a son.

The second word is "reconciliation." This word pictures an estranged child being accepted back into the family. He, too, has no rightful claim to be his son. He depends wholly upon the Father's grace. God's love reaches out to him and embraces him, so he no longer stands outside the circle of the family, but is included in the family.

The third word is "justification." The picture here is that of the guilty person being pronounced innocent. He is guilty, and he is aware of that guilt. "I have sinned," confessed the Prodigal Son. But God, out of His marvelous grace, pronounces the guilty man innocent—because he longs for forgiveness—and deals with him thereafter as if he were innocent. He is restored to the family.[2]

Life today as we know it is too often a drab and ugly affair. Sin removes the bloom from us. In a real sense, sin is another word for ugliness. Greed disfigures our highways with ugly signs, pollutes our rivers, denudes our forests. What happens to our world ecologically often occurs in our relationship with God and with one another. Ugliness replaces beauty. We need to be restored, and words are the means more often than not that allow for that restoration. We need to return with words.

Return with Words

"Take with you words," Hosea counseled. Our tendency is to say, "Take deeds, for actions speak louder than words." "Talk is cheap," we claim. But is it?

I recently heard a song in which God is saying to us, "I missed My time with you." He is referring to our devotional time we spend with Him. On such an occasion we do not present to God deeds but words. Words are essential to a vital relationship. Words are important to God.

We return home to God more than once in our Christian pilgrimages. Too often we find ourselves in a far country longing for the Father's house. At such times we need to remember that we can return home with words. These words need to be sincere, for hypocrisy is not acceptable. The words need to be accurate—no role-playing. They need to be feeling words, for confession is born of humility. The words need to reveal who we are inside, and this requires courage, for our tendency is to hide. Let us return to Him with words.

1. John Powell, *Why Am I Afraid to Tell You Who I Am?* (Allen, Texas: Argus Communications, 1969), 94.

2. Archibald M. Hunter. *Interpreting Paul's Gospel* (Philadelphia: The Westminster Press, 1954), 23.

4

"I'm Somebody!"

While I was driving to Greenville, South Carolina, to the hospital, the individualized license plate on the car in front of me caught my attention. It identified the driver of the car as a nurse. The main message on the license plate, however, was not the establishment of the person's profession but rather how she felt about herself. That feeling was conveyed with two words in bold-faced lettering: "**I'M SOMEBODY.**"

Jesus spent much of His life helping people to be aware of their worth. "Are not two sparrows sold for a penny?" He said, "yet not one of them will fall to the ground apart from the will of your Father. And even the very hairs of your head are all numbered. So, don't be afraid; you are worth more than many sparrows" (Matthew 10:29-31, NIV).

Whenever and wherever Jesus met people He reminded them by word and deed of their importance. Zacchaeus was informed that he, too, was a son of Abraham. The Samaritan woman by Jacob's Well was astonished that Jesus, being a Jew and a man, would converse with her. The thief on the cross was assured of entrance into paradise.

To be able to look at the person in the mirror and to assert, "I'm somebody," is of utmost importance. To feel a sense of worth is to have one's world revolutionalized. Jesus understood that a vital part of saving people has to do with helping them to recognize how He viewed them. "When he saw the crowds, he had compassion on them because they were harassed and helpless, like sheep without a shepherd" (Matthew 9:36, NIV). People were important to Christ, and, because they were important to Him, their sense of self-worth was multiplied. Life is altered when it dawns upon us that we are of notable worth. Certain changes transpire which determine the qualities of our lives.

How We View Ourselves Plays a Vital Role in How We Choose to Spend Our Lives

"An American Indian legend tells about a brave who found an eagle's egg and put it into the nest of a prairie chicken. The eaglet hatched with the brood of chicks and grew up with them.

"All of his life, the changeling eagle — thinking he was a prairie chicken — did what the prairie chickens did.

"He scratched in the dirt for seeds and insects to eat. He clucked and cackled. And he flew in a brief thrashing of wings and flurry of feathers no more than a few feet off the ground. After all, that's how prairie chickens were supposed to fly.

"Years passed. And the changeling eagle grew very old. One day, he saw a magnificent bird far above him in the cloudless sky. Hanging with graceful majesty on the powerful wind currents, it soared with scarcely a beat of its strong golden wings.

"'What a beautiful bird!' said the changeling eagle to his neighbor. 'What is it?'

"'That's an eagle. The chief of the birds,' the neighbor clucked. 'But don't give it a second thought. You could never be like him.'

"So the changeling eagle never gave it another thought. And it died thinking it was a prairie chicken."[1]

How do you see yourself? Do you really believe in you?

Occasionally the writer, just as a form of shock treatment, responds differently from what people expect to given statements. A person may compliment me with "You did a great job," and I will reply, "I know it." Or someone states, "That's a good-looking suit you are wearing," and I respond, "The man makes the suit."

Writing assignments have been a constant companion in my life for twenty-five years. Sometimes when an assignment is completed, and it expresses exactly what I want to say, I get up and walk around the office and say to myself as I do so, "Tip" (my nickname), "that was a great job."

Humility is not self-defacement— rather a recognition that we are indebted to God and others. Feeling good about myself is one avenue for expressing to God and others my deep appreciation for the investment they have made in my life.

Ola Cowing Phillips was one of my favorite teachers. She had a way of making us feel good about ourselves. One happening during my seventh-grade experiences with her still engenders good feelings. We were playing a nearby school in baseball, and I was in center field. The batter hit a ball my way, and running in toward the infield, I reached up and caught it. There was a loud cheer from my classmates. When the inning was over and we came in to bat, Mrs. Phillips looked at me and nodded her head in approval for what I had done. Even now good feelings rise up when I recall that setting.

Our attitudes toward ourselves create the world in which we live. They determine whether or not we spend our lives decrying who we are or affirming our personhood.

How We View Ourselves Conditions How We View Others

When we feel ourselves to be really something special, we can allow others to be something special, too. To arrive at that stage of maturity where we can rejoice with those who rejoice and weep with those who weep is indeed an accomplishment.

Recently a friend was appointed to a prestigious position in our denominational convention. Sorting out my real feelings in regard to the matter, and finding them to be only positive, gave me a sense of pride. So often the feelings we express may be in keeping with what the occasion demands rather than our genuine feelings. As our self-image improves, the success of others does not threaten us, nor does their failure cause us to overly despair. Success and failure are a part of the human scene for us and our friends.

Bruce Larson in his book, *Dare to Live Now,* shares an interesting story which affirms the subject under consideration.

"About a year ago I met a man at a clergy retreat. At the opening meeting tempers got out of hand. Many of us were somewhat edgy and ruffled. This particular man, though not one of the official leaders, was the person who again and again was God's catalyst to change the atmosphere. His humor and insight and honesty were refreshing.

"The next morning at breakfast he walked by my table. I grabbed his hand as he went by and said, 'Trevor, I want you to know that I thank God for you.'

"'Oh, Bruce,' he said smilingly, 'I thank God for myself!'

"I was amazed. I thought, this explains it. He can love others because he loves himself. He has all the troubles we have and is not perfect, but he can love himself because he knows that Jesus Christ loves him and he dares to call himself 'Beloved.'"[2]

An interesting facet of life is that we see others through the window of our own personality. Who we are colors what we view. The thief distrusts because he is a thief. The bigot distorts because he is a bigot. The caring person perceives right motivation because his motives are pure.

My stepmother's opinion of me reached far beyond what I knew myself to be. To her my motives were totally pure. My abilities matched any demand, and my accomplishments far exceeded reality. How did she reach such conclusions? Why did she see me that way? The answer is really simple: she was viewing me through the eyes of her own personality. Who she was colored her perception of me. She saw people at their best. Disparaging remarks were foreign to her. Caring was a way of life. Through those eyes she sized up others, including me.

How We View Ourselves Tempers How We See God

The goal for the Christian life which is most often stated is that we submit ourselves to God, allowing Him to modify our personalities into His image. The truth of the matter is that many times the opposite happens. We make God a projection of our own character. It is not by accident that the authoritarian personality usually gives strong emphasis to the authority of God, and especially of the Bible. Contrariwise the tolerant person stresses the tolerance of God. Appropriate Scripture passages are then chosen to support whichever view one holds.

Subjectivity is a subtle trait. Its first expression is denial. Like the addicted person, admittance of addiction is extremely hard. And yet, like the addicted person, admittance is the first step in recovery or correction. No one of us is totally without the element of subjectivity. It is always a matter of degree. To face up to the truth that even our view of God is tempered by our subjectivity is to become more open to objective tests by which our subjectivity can be altered.

One such test is what is referred to as "approaching the Scripture without presupposition." The common view of this approach is that we come to the Scripture as a clean slate, and let God imprint upon our lives what He wishes to say to us through His Word. Another view seems to be more correct. This approach takes into account the fact that we are not clean slates. Written upon the pages of our lives are all the experiences through which we have gone. Suddenly divesting ourselves of these experiences is impossible. Even God's Spirit begins His work within the parameters of who we are, in order to lead us to new heights of understanding and commitment.

To come to the Scripture without presupposition, then, is to come to it as we are, slates upon which the experiences of life have been written. However, there is one major step here that makes all the difference in the world. That is, we do not declare, before we read the Scripture, what we shall be after we read it. With this approach we are open to change. We still recognize that who we are tends to shape our understanding. But that very recognition gives God's Spirit a better chance to change entrenched patterns of thought and action. Thus, who and what we are, while influencing even how we see God, does not control what we shall become.

Another test to moderate subjectivity is to expose our views to the larger Christian community. The danger here is that we tend to share our concepts only with those who agree with us. A better way is to select some persons with proven integrity and honesty who will lay it on the line for us, thus giving us a wider understanding by which to judge our thoughts and actions. The final decision is ours to make, but we have broadened the base on which those decisions are made.

The sixth beatitude makes an interesting observation (Matthew 5:8). Jesus states that the pure in heart see God. So, seeing God is not a matter of optics but of our spiritual condition. To see God more clearly, then, is to move toward him more nearly. One way to accomplish this goal is to recognize that who we are shapes our view of who He is, but through opening our lives to be changed, we are permitted to see Him more clearly as He is.

In Conclusion

At the conclusion of a worship service the writer was leading, the people were asked to turn to at least one other individual and to say, "I'M SOMEBODY!" It was a heightened time for the worshipers. They were affirming through spoken words the theme for the morning worship. It was obvious that the feeling tone was high. Also, certain inhibitions were discarded for the moment. The prevailing conditions allowed for openness of expression. So, for the first time, many worshipers were sharing in words with another person a deep longing of their hearts, the desire to be somebody.

How we view ourselves is of enormous consequence. It establishes how we live our lives, how we see and relate to others, and how we see and relate to God.

1. "You're Really Something—The Changeling Eagle," *Christopher News Notes*, No. 229.

2. Bruce Larson, *Dare to Live Now*, (Grand Rapids, MI: Zondervan Books, 1965), 21.

5

Talking to Ourselves
Matthew 12:34

A college professor often talked to himself as he walked about on campus. One day a student became brave enough to ask him why. "Well," the professor replied, "there are two reasons. One is that I like to talk to an intelligent person. The other is that I like to hear an intelligent person talk."

All of us perhaps at one time or another have talked to ourselves, though not for the same reasons that the professor did. Speech is a pivotal factor in revealing who we are. This is never more true than when we are talking to ourselves. When talking to others we may withhold words or allow the situation to dictate what we say, but these restraints are somewhat removed when we converse with ourselves. What we say to others is important, but not as revealing as what we say to ourselves.

Various statements have arisen that depict the importance of our words in relating inner character.

"What lies in the well of the heart will come up in the bucket of speech."

"You can judge the wheels a person has in his head by the spokes that come out of his mouth."

"For out of the overflow of the heart the mouth speaks" (Matthew 12:34b, NIV).

In the same way that accent indicates the section of our country in which we grew up, so speech gives evidence of the condition of the heart. When we examine what we say to ourselves. we have a clue as to who we are, and what we are increasingly becoming.

Let us observe a few persons in the Bible who talked to themselves and revealed thereby the inner precincts of their hearts.

The Materialist (Luke 12:16-19)

"And he thought within himself, saying . . . " are words indicating that in talking with ourselves, outward verbalization is not an essential factor. Our words may never be expressed vocally, but that does not diminish their revealing nature.

One characteristic of the materialist is that his universe has a well-defined center, and that center is himself. The pronouns "I" and "my" and "mine" appear often in the rich man's speech. It is quite obvious that "others" are relegated to an insignificant role. It never occurred to the rich man that his present barns might have been adequate had distribution of goods been his theme. But again, there was too much ego in his world for such a radical consideration.

Another characteristic of the materialist is that "life" and "things" are inseparable. To have life one must have things. So, the amassing of wealth becomes dominant in how he governs his life. Every decision is weighed in the light of material gain. If it does not meet the material criteria, it is hastily discarded.

The materialist would not understand Jesus' words that life is not found in the amount of materials one possesses. So, the materialist goes on increasing the amount of his bank account, acquiring more houses and land, and extending his business interests, thinking thereby to find life. When satisfaction does not come with increased possessions, he simply steps up the pace of his activity.

One of the foremost ethical questions that faces us today is, "When is enough, enough?" When our search for life focuses on the accumulation of material things, enough is never enough. The appetite becomes insatiable.

Again, the materialist feels very insecure. When life itself depends primarily upon what one possesses, considering their transitory nature, a sense of insecurity prevails. Our lives are made secure not by things, but by the triumph over things. The test of real life is how much life would we have left if suddenly all material things were swept away.

The Arrogant (Matthew 3:7-10)

"And think not so within yourselves, . . ." indicates again that, in talking to ourselves, the words need not be vocalized. We think in words, and Jesus was able to discern what the Pharisees and Sadducees were saying with their thoughts when they visited where John the Baptist was baptizing. Perhaps their body language, or how they kept their distance, or even the way they observed, clearly indicated that, though they were present in body, they were not present in spirit. Their attitude was out of sync with the occasion. They were arrogant. "We have Abraham to our father. So, why should we listen to some upstart like you?"

The observation has been made that when we don't have anything else to fall back on, we can always fall back on race. Having Abraham as father was the prevailing factor in the equation for the Pharisees and Sadducees.

Now I am quick to assert that there is such a thing as rightful pride. Pride in family, nation, and even accomplishments can have a genuine ring. One evening, when I was strolling across the church yard, my mother, who died when I was five years old, flashed in my mind. It occurred to me that she must have wondered many times during her terminal illness what would happen to me after her death. So, speaking as if my mother were walking alongside me, I said, "Mom, I made it." That experience was a high moment for me. To affirm I had made it didn't mean my accomplishments were greater than what others had attained. In fact, comparisons played no role at the time. It was simply a recognition that some of the dreams a mother would have for her son had been realized. I was happy. My talents were being utilized. God had given me the opportunity to minister in His name. Those accomplishments would have made a mother proud of her son.

There is another type of pride which destroys—arrogance. When a comparison is made in this kind of pride, the one making the comparison always comes out on top. His perspectives, his way of doing things, even his view of God, are without an equal.

This kind of arrogance does destroy. It builds walls in relationships because all other people are considered of a lesser breed. It locks the doors of the heart when truth comes knocking because no additional understanding is needed. The arrogance of God's own people caused them to reject His Messiah. "We have Abraham as our father," they said. The old wineskins — that is, the familiar, the established patterns — were not about to give in to the new and different.

The Repentant (Luke 15:17-19)

"And when he came to himself, he said . . ." are the beginning words in a well-rehearsed speech designed to be delivered to the Prodigal's father upon his arrival back home. The prepared words contain three distinct elements—the Prodigal's present status, his resolve to return home, and a description of his underlying attitude.

Depravity has an insidious way of getting our attention. Especially is this true when one has known better times, and one's present condition is a result of bad choices. Feeding hogs while the hunger pangs gnaw at the stomach has a way of bringing one to his senses. Even the hired servants back home had enough bread to eat and some extra, but the Prodigal was starving. What had begun as a thrilling adventure had turned into a nightmare. The father's house which had once seemed so restrictive had now become so inviting. He wanted to go home.

"I will arise and go to my father . . ." are words that express deep resolve. A decision had been made that called for action; the trip back home was begun without delay.

There are some facets of the journey that will forever remain a mystery. Where the Prodigal strayed to when he left home, and thus the distance of his return trip, are unknowns. One can imagine that he traveled with quickened pace. Perhaps he recited a number of times his prepared speech, but there was one fact about which there was no doubt. The Prodigal was going back home, and nothing was going to stop him.

Attitudes which propel a given action are all-important. Wrong attitudes spoil the action, but right attitudes enhance its meaning. The Prodigal's speech not only depicted his resolve to return home, but his posture as well. "I will arise and go to my father and I will say, I have sinned against heaven and against thee. I am no longer worthy to be called your son." With these words the Prodigal admitted the error of his wayward journey, and the deep feeling of unworthiness regarding any possible restoration.

It should be noted that the Prodigal's words did not include any excuse for his leaving home. "I have sinned." No embellishment. No attempt to give supporting reasons for his wayward action. Genuine repentance tends in the direction of brevity. Wordiness often indicates superficiality. Admitting that we are wrong can be succinctly put.

The feeling that invariably accompanies repentance is a sense of unworthiness. Repentant people readily employ feeling words. To share our feelings with another person digs to the root of our attitude. The Prodigal was en route back home, knowing full well that restoration to sonship within the family was undeserved. He was not worthy of such benevolent treatment.

When we share the feeling that undergirds an action it allows for a meaningful response to that action. Such was the case with the

Prodigal Son. When he expressed his feeling of unworthiness to his father, the father responded with those actions that indicated full acceptance. "Quick," he commanded, "Bring the best robe and put it on him. Put a ring on his finger and sandals on his feet. Bring the fattened calf and kill it. Let's have a feast and celebrate." The lost son had returned, and that was cause for celebration.

The Hopeful (Mark 5:28)

For she said, "If I may but touch his clothes, I shall be whole." These were words of hope spoken by a woman who had been ill for twelve years. Through that time she had suffered much under many doctors and had spent all she had, yet instead of becoming better she grew worse. Nothing saps the spirit more than an extended illness wherein the search for a cure has proved to be futile, but hope does reign eternal. In spite of the past failures, in spite of the nature of her disease, in spite of the crowd around Jesus, in spite of her timidity—she wanted to touch Him and slip quietly away. She weaved herself closer and closer to Jesus until she could reach out and touch His garment, feeling deep in her heart that if she did so, she would be made whole. We call such a resolve hope.

"Being at the end of one's rope" is an expression that has become a familiar part of our language. What that statement depicts is a common experience in life. Life is going along smoothly, and then catastrophe strikes. The unimaginable occurs. Our world caves in. The dreams we had yesterday are shattered. The road ahead appears to be rocky and steep. We are "at the end of our rope."

Then something happens! A little light appears at the end of the tunnel. There is a small break in the dark clouds. The element of hope appears. Perhaps there is a way, after all, to rediscover life. That moment came for the woman with the issue of blood when she heard of Jesus. How she heard we do not know. The important fact is that she did hear and hope reappeared.

One characteristic of hope is that it does not sit idly by. Hope propels us into action. "When she heard about Jesus, she came up behind him in the crowd and touched his cloak, because she thought, 'If I just touch his clothes, I will be healed.'"

The statement has been made that when we are at the end of our rope, we can tie a knot in it. Hope is that knot. Hope keeps us from completely letting go of the rope. It allows us to hang on long enough that alternatives to despair can be considered, and the curative processes

37

of mind and body can begin working. Hope makes it possible for us to discover the greatest of discoveries, and that is: that our touch of desperation claims the attention of Christ Himself. He is both aware of and responds to our call for help. He would not allow the woman to slip away unrecognized and unnoticed.

Conclusion

What we say to ourselves discloses much about ourselves. Our speech reveals both who we are and what we are becoming. Therefore, an evaluation of our words are in order. Just as the doctor examines the tongue to discern diseases of the body, we can examine our words to discover diseases of the heart. What did I say to myself in those unguarded moments is a question that we need desperately to ask ourselves. "For out of the overflow of the heart the mouth speaks."

6

When an Apology Is Out of Order
Luke 15:1-2,25-32

When conflictual situations arise, an explanation is almost always in order, but not always an apology. Luke 15 provides us with an excellent example of such an occurrence. Conflict arose regarding Jesus' association with tax collectors and sinners (Luke 15:1-2). The Pharisees and teachers of the law felt this to be inappropriate action, so they muttered, "This man welcomes sinners and eats with them."

Jesus' response to the criticism came in the form of three stories, each seeking to explain His action (Luke 15). An attempt to explain one's choices when conflict arises is an act of love. It indicates that one cares what others think. People are not written off because they differ in viewpoint, even when that viewpoint may be unjustified. It mattered to Jesus that the religious leaders viewed as abhorrent His association with those they considered undesirables.

However, it would help to note that the attempt to explain did not assume the form of an apology. While an explanation indicates that one cares for others, and wants them to understand a given action, an apology denotes something quite different. Therefore, there are those times when an explanation does not include an apology, as was the case with Jesus in Luke 15.

Then, when is an apology out of order? What does an apology indicate that would make it inappropriate in given circumstances while quite acceptable in others?

An Apology Is Out of Order When . . . It Would Indicate an Intent to Change One's Action When There Is No Plan to Do So

The very basis for an apology is that one has done something wrong or inappropriate and intends to change. The behavior that has caused the conflict will henceforth be avoided. To apologize for one's deportment while vowing to continue on the same course renders an apology useless.

Jesus did not plan to alter His behavior. It was the lost He had come to save. Isolation from those who needed Him was unthinkable. A shepherd would not leave a lost sheep stranded in the wilderness. A woman would not consider a missing coin unimportant. A father would not look on a wayward son as one to be treated with disdain. Neither would Jesus turn away the tax collectors and sinners who gathered around Him to hear Him. He would explain His action, but no apology was forthcoming, because he intended to continue His association with them.

Expanding what we think and feel into a Christian life-style sometimes means continuing an action which others consider inappropriate. Various responses are open to us when this happens. We can ignore the criticism, we can retaliate in kind by responding with criticism, we can apologize, or we can make an honest attempt to explain our action while, at the same time, making it clear that we intend to continue. When the latter course is taken, our reasons must be sound and our purposes clear. Jesus' reason for associating with sinners was that it was through personal contact His message would be heard. His purpose for doing so was that He had come to seek and to save the lost.

An Apology Is Out of Order When . . .
It Would Allow the Other Person to Focus Blame

The manner in which a statement is spoken is often as important in conveying a message as is the statement itself. The words of the older brother, "this son of yours," in verse 30 probably were slanted in such a manner as to cast blame on the father for the younger son's behavior. The implication seems to be, if he were my brother instead of your son, his trek to the far country would not have happened. His approach was much like one parent who, when the child is misbehaving, looks at the other parent and snorts, "He's your son!"

Focusing blame is a common practice when conflict arises. Self-righteous persons—represented by the older brother—tend to find it easy to point fingers. Why? Because their perspective is that "I am right, and you are wrong. Therefore, because you are wrong, you are to be blamed."

Those individuals who press for apologies usually are habitual blamers. Focusing blame on the other person comes easy for them. Their halo shines so brightly that it makes all persons and things around them to appear dark. Casting blame is the natural outgrowth of such an approach to life.

To remain healthy as Christians we need to accept blame when blame is due. Each of us needs an altar at which our sins are confessed and forgiven. However, to allow others to cast blame on us as an accepted pattern, when their goal is to relieve themselves of any blame, is destructive to wholeness. An apology is not to be given when it would allow the other person to focus undeserved blame on us. Our approach again can be to explain our action, but not apologize for it.

An Apology Is Out of Order When . . .
It Would Grant the Other Person the Right to Cast Guilt

Verses 29 and 30 have as their design the casting of guilt by the older son upon the father whose benevolent actions toward his younger son were considered by him to be unfitting. Printed below are the two verses from the *New International Version* with those words underlined which indicate the intent to cast guilt. See if they sound familiar.

"Look! All these years I've been slaving for you and never disobeyed your orders. Yet you never gave me even a young goat so I could celebrate with my friends. But when this son of yours who has squandered your property with prostitutes comes home, you kill the fattened calf for him!"

Perhaps there are other words which you find laden with guilt, for the whole purpose of the statements seems to be to remind the father that he has treated a Prodigal Son better than a loyal one. Such unfitting action should make him feel guilty.

I once attended a conference in which the main thrust of the leader seemed to be on what we don't do that we should be doing. Making us feel guilty for our negligence was his intent. My response was, I refuse to allow another person to pile guilt upon me unnecessarily, for healthy Christians do not enjoy casting guilt on others, nor do they allow others to cast guilt upon them. Our primary goal for life should not be to make others feel guilty—they feel enough guilt without our efforts—but to point them to the One who can free them of inordinate guilt.

Placing guilt upon others can become a mask to conceal our own delinquent behavior. There is little doubt that had the elder son found himself free to join the festive occasion, his tirade against his father would not have occurred. In order to justify his anger and resultant action, he sought to make his father feel guilty.

An Apology Is Out of Order When . . . It Would Allow Another Person to Project His Feelings on You As If They Should Be Your Feelings When They Are Not What You Are Feeling

The elder brother was angry, and he could not understand how any sane human being wasn't angry too (v. 28). How could the return of a Prodigal Son engender joy and call for festivity? The music, the dancing, the banquet table, all were out of keeping with what should be.

Here you have two persons reacting to the same occasion with opposite feelings. One felt joy, the other anger. What made the difference? Does it have to do with how we view waywardness? To the elder brother right was right, and wrong was wrong, and to celebrate one's homecoming who had veered from the right course was unconscionable. To the father right was right, and wrong was wrong also, but to see one coming home who had learned the hard way that right is right, and wrong is wrong, called for celebration and joy, not anger and punishment.

To the elder brother life was staying home, abiding by the rules, and remaining loyal, even when his motivation for doing so may not have been the highest. But the father understood that there is another approach to life which tests the rules and challenges the boundaries as to whether or not they are real. There is risk involved here. One may find himself in a far country, destitute and without friends. But there is hope as well, for while under these dire circumstances, one may "come to himself." He may discover that sin is not just breaking a rule, or leaving home, or wasting one's inheritance in riotous living, but that sin is what denies us the best in life. Sin causes us to be restless when surrounded with the comforts of home. It leads us to demand rights we are not yet ready to receive. It causes us to turn our backs on those who care for us the most as if it doesn't matter. The father was both appreciative of the son who stayed home and the son who returned home because he understood how life works. We find ourselves in different ways, and sometimes we don't find ourselves at all. And neither staying home nor traveling to a far country guarantees "coming to our senses." The father, understanding this, pleaded with his angry son to join the banquet table because the occasion called for joy. A wayward son had come home.

There is the tendency within most of us to dictate the feelings of others on the basis of our own feelings. Different feelings are not to be tolerated because genuine feelings would be the same as ours. When we become aware that another person is projecting his feelings on us as if those feelings are the only response to a given occasion, it is time for us to say "No!" without apology. Feelings are always personal, that is,

I cannot feel for another or another for me. To be aware of my own feelings, and to give them guidance with my best thought, is the wise course.

An Apology Is Out of Order When . . .
It Would Free the Other Person of Responsibility for His Action

Observe what the father didn't say when he went outside the house to plead with his older son to join the family inside the house. He didn't say, "I apologize for the banqueting. It was really a bad idea. I got caught up in the emotion of the occasion and went too far. So, it's OK if you stay out here in the field sulking. I'll get you off the hook. I'll find some excuse for your not being at the party."

No. He went out and entreated him to come in. He explained to the elder brother that the attention the younger son was receiving did not indicate that he loved him more. "My son," a term of endearment, "you are always with me, and everything I have is yours. But we had to celebrate and be glad, because this brother of yours was dead and is alive again; he was lost and is found."

Whether or not the elder brother ever went into the house, the story doesn't tell us. It ends with him still outside. But it is clear that the father wanted him inside. He pleaded with him to join the family. Your brother has come home, and we had to celebrate. Being angry and remaining outside the house didn't befit the occasion.

A quick apology can serve the purpose of relieving another of responsibility for his response to a situation. When this is the case, we can explain our course of action, but withhold an apology. When we feel deeply that our choices were right and our actions correct, we have to stick with them without apology, especially when an apology would free the disagreeing person from responsibility.

An Apology Is Out of Order When . . .
It Would Indicate That the Elements of Grace, Mercy, and Forgiveness, Extended to Another, Were a Mistake

Some prevalent statements would have been appealing to the elder brother in regard to how he felt the younger brother should have been treated upon his return home. "Go for the jugular vein." "Make the rascal pay." "Squeeze the turnip until it bleeds." Occasionally, I am approached by someone who feels that something is awry in the story. Identification with the elder brother's stance is quite common.

Many Christians are still totally Old Testament in their perspective. How often are the words, "an eye for an eye, and a tooth for a tooth," quoted. The "I tell you" of Matthew 5:38-42 is seemingly forgotten, since it speaks of a nobler response than returning in kind.

No one realized better than the Prodigal that the treatment he was receiving was undeserved. "I am no longer worthy to be called thy son" speaks volumes relative to his attitude. The elder brother did not understand that grace, mercy, and forgiveness are not granted on the basis of merit, but on our willingness to receive them. The whole perspective of the cross of Christ is that all of us, because of our sin, deserve to die, and that Christ died in our place. The efficacy of that sacrificial act is granted to us on the basis of grace and our acceptance of it through faith (Ephesians 2:8-9).

The extension of grace, mercy, and forgiveness by the father to his returning son were not the actions of a doting parent, but the responses of one who understood how God deals with us all. The invitation to return home when we have strayed to the far country is forever open. Our acceptance back home is never an earned response, whether we be the son who stayed home and faithfully served, or the one who skipped town. Either way, our acceptance is closely tied to attitude, that is, whether or not we really want to be home. Therefore, the father would explain his benevolent treatment of his younger son to his angry brother, but no apology was forthcoming.

One of the most fascinating aspects of Jesus' life is that He became involved with people on their own turf. To do this takes a lot of honesty in relationships. This type of association tends to reveal what is real and genuine about us. The shallow in us under such conditions cannot remain hidden.

The other approach to relationships in religious circles is to disassociate ourselves from those persons who are different, especially those we consider less committed than we are. A set of standards is developed whereby we can measure accurately who is religious and who is not. This code of conduct usually includes ceremonial religious practices, manner of dress, certain prohibitions, and surely with whom and how we are to relate. "Come ye out from among them and be ye separate" becomes the watchword. Such an admonition is never tempered by the life example of One who must have felt comfortable eating at the table with those whom the religious leaders of His day considered unclean.

Love has a way of breaking down distinctions and propelling us into action when we see people, really see people, as lost and needing a shepherd. Jesus associated with those whom He had come to save.

When criticized for such activity, He would explain why He did it, but no apology was expressed. Hopefully we can have the discernment that allows us to know when, and when not, an apology is needed.

7

God's Will and My Life Attitude? Or Vocation and Location?
Philippians 2:5-11

Finding God's will for our lives is a common theme among Christian people. Usually it is talked about in terms of a particular vocation and area or location. "What is it God wants me to do and where am I to do it?" are the questions most asked.

Every sincere Christian wrestles with both questions. Doing what God wants one to do and where He wants it done is the goal most sought. But there are other questions that need to be asked in relation to "finding God's will."

Does the word "finding" indicate that knowing God's will is somehow difficult? Does God play games with us—now you see it, now you don't? Stories have arisen which seem to indicate that the more difficult God's will is to find, and the greater the struggle in finding it, the more genuine the experience. Is that a true assumption?

Another question which seems always to be kept in the background, if considered at all, is: Does God's will deal primarily with vocation and location? Or does it deal with attitude? Is there a disposition that must precede the choosing of work and place? Does the difficulty in finding our role in God's world center around a misunderstanding of how we are to go about it?

"Don't get the cart before the horse" has relevance to the subject under consideration. We may struggle with vocation and location because we have not first dealt with attitude, for if the attitude is out of kilter, direction will be also.

Philippians 2:5 focuses on attitude. Paul wrote, "Your attitude should be the same as that of Christ Jesus." Then he proceeds to describe Christ's role as it emanated from His attitude (Philippians 2:6-11).

My contention at this point is that a right choice of vocation and location rests upon right attitude. Unless we cultivate the mind-set of Christ, our decisions will be made in the light of factors foreign to the Christian way. Placing emphasis upon attitude rather than majoring on what I am to do and where I am to do it gives a sound basis for a right decision.

Finding God's will for our lives consists more of reading the obvious signs that Christ has placed along the road than it does of having him put up new and unusual ones. Most of the questions we ask are already answered if we read the signs. Sometimes we seek new and unusual signs because we don't like the direction the old signs give us. An examination of the Bible passage in Philippians reveals what these clear road signs are.

The first is condescension. "Your attitude should be the same as that of Christ Jesus; Who, being in very nature God, did not consider equality with God something to be grasped, but made Himself nothing . . . " (NIV). Position often becomes the utmost factor in the making of choices. The maintenance of position becomes everything. How many are willing to make downward moves—or even lateral?

Christ made the greatest downward move of all. "For you know the grace of our Lord Jesus Christ, that though He was rich, yet for your sakes He became poor, so that you through His poverty might become rich" (2 Corinthians 8:9, NIV). This willing condescension was born of His attitude. Disposition preceded mission.

When we stand at the crossroad, and a choice has to be made, does the sign reading condescension seem attractive? Or do we look for a sign of our own choosing? Maybe the signs reading position and power and prestige are more becoming to our goals.

A young man was asked to lead a group of young adults to define success. Materials were given him which explored the various facets of success. All of these were ignored in the discussion. The primary goal of success to the leader was to be number one, not two, or three, or four. Such goals as happiness, wholesome friendships, and feeling good about one's work were secondary in importance.

The point being made here is not that an upward move is always wrong. When that is our goal, however, without other considerations, it is time to take a close look at the sign reading condescension.

There are times when position allows for greater service. A given location may best fit our talents. Reading the clear road sign marked condescension will not violate the goal of usefulness—but will enhance it. We need to remember that it was through condescension that Christ fulfilled His role in God's plan.

Another road sign is servanthood. Jesus took "the very nature of a servant" (Philippians 2:7). A part of Jesus' servant role was that He donned human likeness. He had a body that grew tired. He became hungry and thirsty; He could feel physical and emotional pain; He could be hurt, even killed, by angry hands. Sure, there were opposite times as well, but the disparity between the divine and the human became His lot. Heaven's precincts were surrendered willingly for earth's toils.

Jesus' life on earth became a model of servanthood. When new and dynamic truth is to be presented, modeling, not only teaching, is the necessary avenue for dissemination. People can better understand when they see it done. So, Jesus' earthly sojourn began in a modest home and culminated on a cross. The time between was marked by numerous examples of servanthood.

The disciples, like ourselves, often became caught up in evaluating greatness in terms of the standards of society at large. Would they sit in the place of honor in His kingdom? Who would be greatest among them? The rivalry even led to the avoidance of menial tasks. They needed a model to show them what true greatness really is. So, Jesus took a towel and basin of water and washed their feet. Here was the One they called Lord doing what servants did. And then, to drive home the truth, He said, "Do you understand what I have done for you? You call me 'Teacher' and 'Lord,' and rightly so, for that is what I am. Now that I, your Lord and Teacher, have washed your feet, you also should wash one another's feet. I have set you an example that you should do as I have done unto you" (John 13:12-15, NIV).

Great truths, if taken seriously and applied diligently, would revolutionize how we live. Imagine with your wildest dream what drastic changes could occur in church life if we defined greatness as servanthood. The pastor might occupy a smaller and less elaborately furnished office than other staff members. The church administrator might work a day as custodian to allow an overworked custodial person a day off. Salaries might be reversed so that those who do the menial tasks receive the highest pay. Unthinkable! Yes. Because our standards for greatness are set by the world's standards of greatness.

Recently, a husband and wife were retired early because of a downsizing of the labor force at the company where they had been employed for many years. Both individuals have filled prominent roles in their church. The husband has served more than once as a deacon chairman. The wife has played an important role as a committee person.

When the couple, my friends and former parishioners, took the job as custodians at their church, I could not have been more proud of them. My appreciation level leaped upward even from the high level formerly held. Great truths are more easily talked about than lived, but when we see them applied in life they are something to behold.

Christ's role emanated from a right understanding of servanthood. To wash the disciples' feet did not diminish His personhood but rather enhanced it. When making decisions about the course of our lives, we need to read closely the road sign marked servanthood. The signs marked prestige, honor, and position belong to another realm.

A third road sign is humility. "And being found in appearance as a man, he humbled himself . . ." (Philippians 2:8a). Humility has to do not only with accepting a given role but how we feel about that role as well. Jesus' condescension into the role of servanthood did not leave Him embittered. Because of His attitude He could readily accept that function as God's plan for His life. The writer of Hebrews puts it succinctly. "Let us fix our eyes upon Jesus, the author and perfecter of our faith, who for the joy set before him endured the cross, scorning its shame, and sat down at the right hand of the throne of God. Consider him who endured such opposition from sinful men, so that you will not grow weary, and lose heart" (Hebrews 12:2-3).

Humility is a feeling that cannot be conjured up, or else it will be unreal. It is a by-product of a predisposition. To become aware that one has it is to lose it. Jesus' humility was born of His attitude. Fulfilling the Father's assignment for His life was not degrading or shameful to Christ because of an attitude which included humility. His eyes were fixed upon the assignment—therefore He could scorn the shame.

Right decisions regarding God's will for our lives must pass the road sign marked humility. Our eyes need to be fixed on God's task for us, not the observations others may have relative to that role. Right attitude permits us the privilege of centering our efforts on the job at hand rather than using up our energies with concern about how others view us.

Humility has been defined as "strength under control." It is not walking around with drooped shoulders so as to give the appearance of being humble. It springs from a sense of indebtedness to God and others for their investment in our lives. It is commitment to a goal accompanied by a feeling of unworthiness. It is the recognition that our accomplishments are not singularly attained. What and who we are is all wrapped up with others.

One intriguing facet of Jesus' ministry is His recognition that God's ultimate plan included the employment of many people. He alone would not complete that mission. What He began was committed to His disciples to carry on. They in turn would enlist others to be links in the ever-lengthening chain of God's mission. Attitude, particularly the attitude of humility, not only makes one feel good about his role, but allows for a recognition of the importance of other people.

Our state of South Carolina is involved at this time in a program entitled "Empowering Kingdom Growth." The effort includes in part the discovery of individuals with given talents, enlisting and training them for service, and then empowering them to do their job. The empowering element is interesting. It includes a recognition of the gifts of others, a willingness to entrust them with a task, and then getting out of the way so they can do it. The attitude of humility permits this to occur, because then we don't care who receives credit. Our only concern is that the job gets done.

A fourth road sign is obedience. "He became obedient unto death, even death on a cross" (Philippians 2:8b).

Obedience can sometimes be a harsh word. The tone of the voice in which it is spoken, and the circumstances in which it is used, determine the nature of the word. The pointing finger and the demanding voice make the word obedience take on an obnoxious connotation. "You obey me! No questions asked," is an approach that leads to both ineffectiveness and rebellion.

Obedience, on the other hand, can be an attractive, wholesome word. It is no less demanding in this form. In fact, the requirements involved may be even greater. The difference is that, in its attractive form, obedience has been approached from a different angle as to demand, and has taken into account considerations which make its fulfillment a stronger possibility.

In its attractive, wholesome form, obedience is approached as consultation, not as cold, calculated demand. The Bible presents God as the good Father. What "good" parent addresses a child with rabid demand when a decision is to be made? How does the good parent ignore the input of the one who is to carry out the action involved in the decision? Doesn't the good parent know that motivation is heightened when one's views are factored in? God may be a lot of different things to a lot of different people, but He is not dumb. He made us with minds to think and with feeling to express emotion. Why would a wise God ignore how He made us when it comes to understanding the role of obedience in our lives?

It was a red-letter day for me when I came to see obedience as consultation. God and I sit down together as Father and son and discuss together the direction my life should take. There are no "pointing fingers" and "rabid demands," but two persons who love one another talking together in calm voices and with resolute purpose about future plans. Whether to obey or not to obey is not the issue. The goal is to discover as Father and son the most meaningful and purposeful course for my life.

Obedience as consultation is always connected with a goal. It has nothing to do with obedience for obedience's sake. A course of action is decided upon because it accomplishes something. Christ's death, the crowning example of obedience, had purpose and design. Without reason His death would be a gross travesty.

When obedience is connected to a goal the obedience itself takes on meaning. The bumps along the way are endured because one's eye is on the goal. The manner in which Christ spoke His last saying on the cross, "It is finished," is open to conjecture. My personal observation is that it had the sound of triumph. A goal had been attained at the steepest of prices. Obedience had reaped its highest reward, the completion of a worthy task.

Obedience as consultation considers talent, opportunity, and need. One latent fear held by many people is that God's will is somehow connected with making us do what we do not want to do. Again, let the question be asked, "Why would God imbue us with certain gifts, and then ask us to do a work that does not employ those gifts?" Happiness and joy are a result of doing what we do well. So, obedience when related to talent, is no longer a chore. It becomes a privilege. God is not in the business of placing square pegs in round holes. Jesus came to make life whole. A part of wholeness is discovering our gifts and employing them in kingdom service.

Opportunity and need are considerations to be looked at in healthy obedience. What gain is made in choosing a given direction where the doors of opportunity are closed or where there is no need to be met? That is why consultation is so vital. It is not that God doesn't already know where opportunity and need lie. It is that the one seeking the road of obedience doesn't know. And, after all, he is the one who will carry out the implications of the final decision. God will be present in the mission, but He works through human instrumentality.

When our attitude is in keeping with all the road signs, mentioned before and later, and we find the answer to the question, "What do I want to do most?" we will not be very far from the will of God.

51

A fifth road sign is sacrifice. "And being found in appearance as a man, he humbled himself and became obedient to death, even death on a cross" (Philippians 2:8).

I pointed out earlier that modeling is one of the most effective forms of teaching. Jesus' life was a model of sacrifice. It began with His condescension, His coming to earth, and ended with the cruelest of deaths, crucifixion. Describing His own life-style Christ said, "Foxes have holes and birds of the air have nests, but the Son of Man has no place to lay his head" (Luke 10:58).

Softness as a way of life was foreign to Jesus. Perhaps one of the crucial areas of the present age is that the amount of material things we possess has made us soft. Enough never seems to be enough. It never is for spoiled people.

A little girl defined sacrifice as giving up something you can't do without. It is the written-in cost for reaching a given goal. Sacrifice in itself is not the goal. The goal is the goal. Sacrifice is the price one pays to cross the finish line.

While I was serving as pastor in a college community, association with the football players was almost a daily occurrence. A common saying of theirs was, "No pain, no gain." The exercises necessary to get their bodies fine tuned were both demanding and painful. If they did not pay the price in preparation, it would become obvious on the day of the game. One player who often led in prayer prior to the game would pray, "Lord, help us not to half-step today." It was his way of saying that when the game is over, "let it be said we laid it all on the line."

There is little doubt that the value of a given attainment is determined by what it cost. No pain, no gain. Once when a young minister questioned my view of the Bible, there was consolation in recalling what I had written on the fly leaf to my Greek New Testament years earlier. It was in the form of a pledge and said simply, "I desire to be able to share truthfully this book. In order to be able to do so, I will make any sacrifice and will pay any price."

When decision is to be made regarding God's will for us, the cost involved must not be the governing factor. When we have something to live for, we need less to live on. Material convenience is nice to have, but it should not control us. Softness is fast becoming one of our favorite sins. Every one of us for sure is a product of his own generation. Sleeping three in a bed in an unheated house long before air-conditioning came on the scene characterized my boyhood. Indoor plumbing was still in the distant future. When taking a shower even today, I reserve the amount of water by turning it on only to wet the body, and then to rinse off. The plea being made here is not for a return to "the good old days." They were not all that good. The call is for a return to the type of decision-making that is uncalculating.

The symbol of the Christian way remains a cross. Retaining the significance of that symbol is a challenge to all. Especially is this true when making choices regarding God's will. The cost involved often determines which clothes we purchase, the cars we buy, the neighborhood in which we live. Not so with God's will. Jesus' call to those who would follow Him is not to be altered. "If any man will come after me, let him deny himself, and take up his cross daily, and follow me" (Luke 9:23).

The sixth and last road sign is love. Christ said, "If you love me, keep my commandments" (John 14:15). The foundation upon which Christian service rests is love. The motivating force underlying Christian obedience is love. It is the wrapping paper that makes the whole package of doing God's will attractive. A loveless Christian doing his duty can turn off almost everyone with whom he comes in contact. But works of love are attractively done and possess a contagious element.

One incident from my boyhood still engenders good feelings when I recall it. A group of men and children were working in the barn loft at wheat-threshing time. One man sought to raise an altercation with another man. Both were from the church which I attended. The man who initiated the quarrel was quite abusive in tone and language. The other man responded with dignity and respect. He handled the stressful situation so attractively that it impressed me deeply. Even now the very spot in the barn loft where the incident occurred is imprinted in my memory. Works attractively done have that effect. Their influence is like an ever-flowing stream.

Joe and Janet Walker serve as greeters prior to Sunday School in the main lobby at our church. Watching them perform is an object lesson of love in action. Their arrival time is 9:30 a.m., fifteen minutes before Sunday School begins. Meeting this time schedule with two small children is not easy. But to do the work as a greeter makes meeting that time schedule necessary. Joe and Janet do so gladly. Joe, as greeter, does the extra things to make people feel wanted and important. He scurries to open a car door where someone needs assistance. He walks the senior adults to the elevator, very often accompanying them to the desired floor level. Janet meanwhile stands by the door, sometimes with a small baby in arms and the other child in tow, making the people feel welcome. When the road sign marked love guides our actions, they are attractively and contagiously done.

Obedience to God's will is born out of relationship, and relationship is based upon love. Doing God's will is a privilege, not a burden, when we love Christ. Jesus testified concerning His own obedience, "My food is to do the will of him who sent me and to finish his work" (John 4:34). Jesus lived to please God. Pleasing God did not diminish his joy, but rather brought it to full flower.

The thesis for this chapter has been that when we wish to discern God's will for our lives, we need to focus on attitude rather than vocation and location, for when our attitude is Christian our choice of work and place will fall naturally in line. Contrariwise, if we major on vocation and location, ignoring the clear road signs which God has placed along the way, our choice of work and place will be made for the wrong reasons. Cultivating Christ's attitude precedes choice of direction. The means for attaining this attitude is described in Romans 12:2, "Don't let the world squeeze you into its mold, but let God remake you so that your whole attitude of mind is changed" (*Phillips* Translation).

8

Prejudice: The "Acceptable" Sin

Most groups develop a list of what are termed "bad sins," while other equally vicious acts are ignored. To belong to a family clan, a religious denomination, a given race, or a political party is to learn that what is considered good or bad varies greatly from group to group. What is quite acceptable in one setting is deplored in another.

To escape a restrictive and limited view of what sin is consumes time, courage, and openness. The recognition that our concepts of right and wrong were set early, and were arrived at on the basis of group consciousness rather than personal discovery, is to be permitted to re-examine where we stand. Openness is not without its trauma. Risk becomes a factor. But the freedom that prevails when one is willing to examine existing patterns of behavior in the light of fundamental Christian truths is worth all the struggle involved. To be unafraid to walk hand and hand with Christ as He leads us through the gates in the fences which would limit right understanding and restrict appropriate action is both thrilling and comforting.

The topic for this chapter was chosen because among our "worst-sins list," prejudice is usually not included. Even within the Christian community it is often practiced without being challenged. Sermons dealing with our unwarranted views of those who belong to another group are few and far between. The danger level in dealing with the subject of prejudice is high, because people are never more hostile than when their perverted views of others are pointed out.

The arrangement for this chapter is to take certain statements relative to the nature of prejudice, and to comment briefly on what I feel those statements mean. When and where the material was collected has long been forgotten since it occurred over a number of years.

Prejudice Is a Sin Which Everyone Denounces and Almost No One Seriously Confesses

If a list were prepared of ethical issues confronting us on which was listed prejudice, and instructions were given to check those issues we consider most urgent, a large number of people would readily check prejudice. Denouncing prejudice is almost a national pastime, but bashing and recognition of personal guilt are different matters. Denouncing sin in others seldom leads to confession of one's own guilt.

Even the recognition of a sin in general does little until it becomes specific. Prejudice, for example, at large must become prejudice in particular. Only when we see wrong being harmful in a specific way, so that we can touch it, does it take on personal significance.

Serious confession follows recognition of personal guilt. Without recognition there is nothing to confess. Recognition comes when we stare at prejudice not as a sin from which we are isolated, but as a sin in which we participate. The only differences between us are the degree of involvement and the amount of recognition. Those two factors are determined by one's level of sensitivity, not our innocence. When we become aware that prejudice is a sin in which all of us to some degree are involved, then we are ready for serious confession.

Prejudice Has a Profile of Blind Animosity Which, While Seeing What It Pleases, Cannot See What Is Plain

Certain statements have arisen in our language which indicate that we do not always see what is obvious. These are:

"If it had been a snake, it would have bit you."

"It was right before your eyes."

"You wouldn't see it if it hit you in the face."

What we see is governed more by who we are than sharpness of vision. For one thing we see what we want to see. So, whether or not something pleases us plays a role in whether or not we see it. Blotting out what we find to be unacceptable or painful is a common trait.

Also, we can only see what our lives have prepared us to see. Blindness is not always chosen. It comes about many times because we do not have the background that allows us to see. An artist looking at a picture sees intricacies of detail which would go unnoticed by the untrained eye.

How we feel about an issue colors our vision as well. When our feelings are positive about an event or a person, the good aspects receive top consideration. Conversely, when our attitude is negative, the bad points prevail.

Prejudice has a profile of blind animosity, that is, it chooses to see what it pleases, and ignores what is obvious or plain. Blind animosity is a dangerous course. On the one hand it is dangerous because, choosing to see only what it pleases, every issue is distorted. Tunnel vision rules the day. On the other hand it is dangerous because when you add to blindness the emotion of animosity, a lethal combination is created. At its extreme form, it rages. To eradicate or destroy becomes its goal. It is no longer willing only to defeat, it must punish as well.

The observation has been made that a rebel never sees both sides of an issue. If he did, he might not be a rebel. Impartial judgment is a rare commodity. Attaining some degree of objectivity is not easy, because objectivity is a learned art, and no one is perfect at it. Our goal, therefore, is to be aware that all of us color issues on the basis of who we are, and to bring to bear on our opinions certain tests which will lead to sharper clarity of vision.

The "Courage of My Conviction" Is a Fancy Title Many Bigots Give to Their Prejudices.

The bigot is defined as one who is obstinately and intolerantly devoted to his own church, party, belief, or opinion. He does not yield to reason or argument. When his beliefs are challenged, he digs in, in spite of the amount or quality of evidence stacked against him. The truth is he seems to enjoy the fight, because it is the heat of battle on which he thrives most, and it serves as the fuel with which the intensely burning flame of his inner life is stoked.

Carefully and cleverly chosen titles are the weapons with which the bigot fights. These titles are most effective, for they are usually emotionally based, and a large segment of society had rather be stirred emotionally than mentally. Each fancy statement with frequent usage over a period of time picks up a definitive meaning given to it by the way it is used, when it is used, where it is used, and by whom it is used. Closely following a grasp of the meaning of the fancy title, there develops a patterned response to it. It may be the clapping of the hands or a loud chorus of amens. Thus the bigot has accomplished his goal. He has been able to project his views upon masses of people and has engendered their response as he planned it to be.

To have courage that allows us to live out our convictions is noble. What we believe we should live. However, convictions need to have the flexibility that allows us to change course when they no longer fit what we believe. Adjustment and alteration indicate strength, not weakness. We have the courage to change. To say that we have stood on a conviction for years, as if the amount of time alone somehow validates the belief, is not a well-founded position.

The "courage of my conviction" serves as a good example of a broad statement which is often used with an ulterior motive. The obvious connotation is that here we have a person who not only has convictions, but also has the courage to live them. How admirable! Having solicited a favorable response the master of deception can move on to project with cunning skill his perverted views upon his listeners.

Choosing to employ a fancy title somehow indicates a lack of firm basis for the statement. Even more, it may indicate we have something to hide. Why not just talk about the issue at hand with open and honest dialogue? This approach avoids any attempt to overpower, or to deceive—only to understand.

Herein lies the crux of the matter. The bigot cannot afford open and honest communication lest his prejudices be revealed. Having determined to continue as he is—unchanged—he must engage in deception to accomplish his goal of converting others to his way of thinking. Fancy titles are his most effective weapons.

Many People Mistake Thinking for a Rearranging of Their Prejudices

"A man sat before the fireplace in his club, seemingly wrapped in thought. Two friends looked at him, and one said, 'Jones is thinking very deeply tonight.' The other man, who knew Jones more intimately, replied, 'Jones thinks he is thinking, but he is merely rearranging his prejudices.'"[1]

Prejudicial thinking usually follows a circular course. It goes round and round, always returning to the same spot. Whatever expansion that occurs merely enlarges the circle. Any break in the circular fence is promptly repaired lest something new or different invade. There is an intellectual and emotional blindness that occurs which deludes a person by causing him to think that his thoughts are sound, correct, and superior. It is always the other person who is off base.

Healthy thinking, on the other hand, follows more of a straight line. It moves toward a given destination. Today's thought patterns prove inadequate for tomorrow's journey because one has moved farther on the trail. Often the movement forward is like a path winding through the woods. Barriers that would hinder the forward thrust have to be sidestepped or conquered. Immovable objects like trees have to be gone around, and uncrossable streams have to be bridged. But always the movement is forward, though the pace may vary.

Real thinking moves out. Discovery and venture are its themes. It treads where others have not trod and re-energizes what has been. Unwarranted, restrictive boundaries are discarded for open spaces, for real thinking cannot be hemmed in.

Sound thinking is disciplined, for meaningful goals cannot be reached through sloppy thought. Honesty and genuineness constitute the criteria that must be met for continuance in a given direction. Movement alone is not satisfactory. The ultimate destination is given top consideration as choices are made.

The writer, for many years, has received the *Christopher News Notes*. One copy was entitled, "Thoughts on Thinking." To conclude this segment, let me share an extract from that particular pamphlet which defines a thinking person.

A Thinking Person

A thinking person is guided by the facts, no matter how unpalatable they may be.

One who is ruled by emotions often stumbles before reaching the goal.

A thinking person realizes that the right way and the expedient way are not always the same.

One who seeks shortcuts does so at the expense of time, trouble and conscience.

A thinking person learns from the mistakes of others, without rejoicing in their failures.

One who finds fault but does not learn is likely to repeat others' errors.

A thinking person considers the personalities and feelings of others in searching for solutions.

One who is insensitive can be correct in theory but inept in practice.

A thinking person knows when to speak and when to keep silent; when to act and when to wait.

One who is rash or impetuous plunges ahead without any sense of timing.

A thinking person is humble enough to acknowledge wisdom in others.

One who is merely clever feels he has nothing to learn from others.

A thinking person is careful in the use of words.

One who is careless relies on slogans, labels or half-formed opinions.

A thinking person admits that reality is greater than the sum total of his own experiences.

The unthinking makes self the measure of the universe.[2]

Prejudice Is a Great Timesaver . . . It Enables a Person to Form an Opinion Without Bothering to Get the Facts

"Give me your quick opinion" are familiar words for they are used quite often in our "make-haste" society. Quick foods, quick services, quick decisions, quick everything seem to be our theme. That pace fits well with the prejudicial mind-set, because then the time and effort needed to have an accurate base for our opinions can be avoided. When one has already made up his mind, and has no intention of changing it, regardless of the facts, why bother to muddy the water with additional insight?

Arriving at opinions too soon is a malady of our age. Right opinions demand sound, constructive thinking—factual, flexible, and principled. Getting in a hurry undermines all three of the above.

Opinions need to be based upon the best information available. They need to be factual. Sifting out accurate information demands time.

Even facts are interpreted in accordance with our views. Subjectivity is always a factor to be reckoned with. In the prior segment in this chapter, a thinking person is described as one who is guided by the facts, no matter how unpalatable they may be. His is not ruled by emotions. The prejudicial person is inclined to violate both of these guidelines.

Again, opinions need to be flexible, for additional information may lead to a change of sentiment. Our concept of others need not be set in cement. "Now that I know you, I have a different opinion of you," are words common to all of us. A choice statement relative to the matter at hand is that "a person must be big enough to admit his mistakes, smart enough to profit from them, and strong enough to correct them." Flexibility allows us to do just that in regard to our opinions.

Furthermore, opinions need to be guided by sound principles. We should proceed with care when evaluating another individual. Carelessness and recklessness are bed partners.

Being sensitive to the feelings of others constitutes principled action. How others view us is important, because relationships are important. Relationships are based upon deep feelings. Hasty and unfounded views about our personhood can hurt, and hurt intensely.

Caring is another element in principled living. The words "without bothering" in this statement about prejudice really do "bother" me. They indicate that one does not care enough to spend time enough to glean facts enough to form a right opinion. When we care it "bothers" us when views are expressed with little basis for doing so. After all, God gave us hearts, but left it up to us to keep them warm or let them grow cold.

How would we like others to form their opinions about us is another sound principle. Hastily? Deliberately? Well-founded? Most of us would be quick to say, "Take the necessary time to get adequate facts, sprinkle in the element of grace, and then, and only then, arrive at an opinion.

Trying to Reason One Out of His Prejudices Is Folly, Since He Wasn't Reasoned into Them

Exiting a home through the same door that it was entered lest bad luck come our way is a familiar superstition. But, when it comes to ingrained prejudices, that is exactly what has to happen. The door through which biases enter our lives is basically an emotional one, and it is primarily through that same entrance that they are extricated.

Imagine a family sitting together at the evening meal conversing with one another about the fundamental reasons that justify prejudice. Such a conversation would ensue only after the invasion of prejudice, for sound reasoning is not the gateway through which prejudices come. Our biases are developed through being exposed to persons, over an extended period of time, who exhibit strong emotional tones relative to how they feel toward certain groups or individuals. A simpler way of putting it is that prejudice is caught more than it is taught. Constant exposure to prejudicial feelings, especially at a young age, causes them to become ingrained so that disentanglement is very difficult.

Since prejudice is arrived at primarily through the gateway of emotion, it is through that same door that they must be approached if our confrontation is to be effective. Giving a hundred sound reasons why prejudice is unjustified will make little headway. Our beginning point, then, is not why a person thinks as he thinks but why he feels as he feels. It is through identification of the feelings that underlie our biases, and a tracing back step by step of how we arrived at those feelings, that we are allowed the possibility of freedom. We must feel our way out of prejudice just as we felt our way into it.

As stated earlier, relationships form the basic foundation from which we learn. They also constitute the source for our unlearning. Just as continued contact with prejudicial persons tends to promote prejudice, even so constant association with those free of prejudice leans toward liberation. The writer, like many of you, grew up in a time and community where prejudice was an accepted practice. It was the way things were. They had been that way a long time. If you belonged to a certain race you ate at the last table. You observed certain courtesies. It was only later as an adult that the writer became exposed to the person of Jesus Christ. Sitting at His feet led to unlearning certain ingrained feelings. It brought about a drastic change in behavior. It took time, but it worked. That God is no respecter of persons took root.

To close this section a word needs to be said regarding the destructiveness of mass prejudice. When prejudice saturates a nation, or a clan, or a family, it builds up tremendous power. The pressure on the individual to go along, to fit in, is almost unbearable. Those on the periphery tend to be sucked in. To assert ones's desire to travel a different road is viewed as unpatriotic, a denial of the clan, disloyalty to the family. Add to these factors the political, economic, and social implications surrounding our biases, and you have power exemplified. Little wonder then that prejudice becomes an acceptable sin.

Believing That Prejudice Will Work Itself Out If Given Time Is Like Believing That Weeds Will Uproot Themselves of Their Own Initiative

"Let sleeping dogs lie," or "don't make waves," are common approaches used when dealing with prejudice. If left alone, it will somehow go away. But prejudices are like weeds in the garden. Unless they are dealt with—that is, uprooted—they take over the garden.

Any gardener is aware that weeds seem to be sturdier and more prolific than the food-producing plants. When left undisturbed by the gardener, they are going to win over the good plants. It is only through proper preparation of the soil and careful cultivation that the desired results in gardening are achieved. Weeds will not uproot themselves. They have to be confronted.

Some things do not go away with time. Prejudice fits that category. One would think that we would have learned by now that prejudice is a dead-end street. But it rages on with deeper intensity and wider span than ever before.

Confrontation is commonly viewed as a course to be avoided, or at best chosen only as a last resort. It does have its unpleasant side, and very often is downright dangerous. It tests relationships; it involves risk; it demands patience. It is also necessary if changes are to occur. Put briefly, prejudice has to be confronted. It will not go away on its own.

Recently the writer discovered a new word. It is called care-fronting. It includes both caring and confronting.

David Augsburger in his book *Caring Enough to Confront* defines care-fronting for us:

> Care-fronting is offering genuine caring that bids another grow. (To care is to welcome, invite and support growth in another.)
>
> Care-fronting is offering real confrontation that calls out new insight and understanding. (To confront effectively is to offer the maximum of useful information with the minimum of threat and stress.)
>
> Care-fronting unites love and power. Care-fronting unifies concern for relationship with concerns for goals. So one can have something to stand for (goals) as well as someone to stand with (relationship) without sacrificing one for the other, or collapsing one into another. Thus one can love powerfully and be powerfully loving. These are not contradictory. They are complementary.[3]

Care-fronting seems to be a wise and effective approach when challenging prejudice. We care enough to try to understand why prejudices form a part of life. People are not readily discarded because they are biased. Love is not conditional.

But, at the same time, our goal for bringing about desired changes keeps us from sitting idly by while people around us are taken advantage of. We choose the time and place to confront, but we do confront. We employ wisdom in our approach, because we want to be effective. So much attention is given to the "how" we confront.

One of the Greatest Things We Can Do for Our Children Is Not to Pass Our Prejudices On to Them

An almost universal desire on the part of parents is to make life easier for their children than was their own lot. Very often this desire centers in the area of material things. Even a better education may be talked about primarily in terms of getting a better job with more pay. However, the greatest legacy of all may have little to do with houses, lands, cars, or other material amenities, but with an atmosphere where people are valued as people. To be reared in a home where respect for others is both taught and practiced is the greatest legacy of all. To become aware of our own prejudices, and to make a conscious choice not to pass them on to our children, is the best gift possible.

Every child is born free of prejudice. It is through socialization that attitudes are developed. The atmosphere in the home plays a major role as to what those attitudes will be. It is impossible to hide our true values from our children. They see us in good and bad times. They observe what we talk about, how we spend our money, what we give time to, how we feel about events and people.

Our unguarded moments are perhaps the most telling of all as to who we are. This writer's sense of honesty came not as the result of a lecture by my father on the subject, but while watching him measure wheat without the buyer being present. The half bushel container was always "heaped up" a little. Perhaps the buyer knew my father and understood that he would not take advantage of him.

What we say and do in our unguarded moments are what our children catch. They know these are the genuine times. When we intentionally try to influence, it is less effective, because it is less real. So a part of passing on a legacy to our children free of prejudice is to rid our lives of those prejudices passed on to us.

1. Walter Dudley Cavert, *Remember Now* (Nashville: Abingdon-Cokesbury Press, 1944), 202.

2. "Thoughts on Thinking," *Christopher News Notes*, New York, 1972.

3. David Augsburger, *Caring Enough to Confront* (Ventura, CA: Regal Books, 1983), 10.

9

How Big Is Your World?

Giving a baccalaureate address is not always an easy assignment. All too often such speeches are classified as boring and unproductive. My goal was to avoid both pitfalls as I prepared for that address at the local high school.

The graduation exercises were special this year, and my involvement was not the only reason, for among the graduates was our daughter, Joan. So, there was extra incentive to be sure that my part would be both interesting and worthwhile.

I chose a topic in the form of a question — "How Big is Your World?" It is an interesting question that can be answered in many ways. The size of our world could be viewed in terms of land space, population density, or cultural opportunity. But there was another approach to answering the question which intrigued me. It was that the size of our world is not decided entirely by land space, population density, or cultural opportunity, but that our attitudes play a large role. Therefore, inside factors, not merely the matters without, help decide the size of our world.

"What attitudes then," you may ask, "determine the boundaries of our world?" Let us focus our attention on the fundamental attitudes that are present in the lives of those persons whose world is constantly expanding.

Our World . . . As Big As Our Love — As Small As Our Hate

There are times when our minds and hearts are open to some new understanding which afterwards alters our lives forever. Such was the case when the church administration professor made an observation about life that was new and dynamic. He commented, "I refuse to allow anyone to make my world a smaller place in which to live by causing me to hate him." There it was, truth in a nutshell. To allow ourselves to hate diminishes the size of our world, for when we hate even one person, we exclude that person from the inclusiveness of love. To hate, then, is to chip away at the size of our world.

Much of the criticism Jesus faced came from the religious leaders who resented His all-inclusive love. "And the Pharisees and scribes murmured, saying, This man receiveth sinners, and eateth with them" (Luke 15:2).

Love has a way of crossing formidable barriers and climbing almost unscalable walls to reach out to those beyond the fences set up by all-too-common hatreds. God loves the whole world, and Jesus, by His very life-style, lived out that truth amid the restrictive patterns of His day. He touched with love the untouchables. He opened the gates of the "hate fences" of His day and invited those considered to be unworthy to come inside.

Timothy Caleb, a chihuahua, lived in our house as an integral part of the family for almost thirteen years. Timothy had a tremendous capacity for love. Like most dogs he greeted you at the door, teased you to carry him on his daily walks, and let you know by tapping the door when he wanted to go outside. He always wanted to be near you. He would sleep scrunched up to your leg with what appeared to be perfect contentment.

Timothy also had the capacity to hate. When he was small, a big dog jumped on him, and Timothy never forgot. Some dogs, even big ones, he loved. Other he despised. We never knew quite how he made the distinction.

One day new neighbors moved in next door to us. They had a big, black dog named Jim. We called him "Big Jim." Timothy disliked Big Jim almost immediately. Even though Big Jim was inside a fence, it proved to be no barrier to his desire for the outside. He roamed the community. So before we would carry Timothy outside, we had to scan the yard to be sure Big Jim wasn't around. Timothy had to be guarded from Big Jim, even though he didn't think so. Many times he didn't get to go into the yard or on his walk to the city park because Big Jim was outside. If Timothy had been content to let Big Jim be, he could have avoided many a skirmish. But his dislike for Big Jim just had to come out. I tried to explain to Timothy that his dislike for Big Jim was limiting his own activity, but being a dog, he couldn't understand that. But we as human beings ought to understand it. Hating someone is like burning down our house in order to get rid of a rat. Hate destroys the hater. Hate decreases the size of our world.

Martin Luther King, Jr., wrote in his book *Stride Toward Freedom,* "To retaliate in kind would do nothing but intensify the existence of hate in the universe. Along the way of life, someone must have sense enough and morality enough to cut off the chain of hate."

The observation has been made that "every bigot was once a child free of prejudice." We must learn to pass on to our children our "loves" so they will not have to overcome the barriers with which we had to deal. Then the size of their world, as is ours, will be determined by their love and not their hate.

Our World . . . As Big As Our Service — As Small As Our Selfishness

Jesus, in defining His ministry, said, "For even the Son of man came not to be ministered unto, but to minister, and to give His life a ransom for many" (Mark 10:45, KJV). Greatness in the kingdom of God is decided on the basis of service (see Mark 10:42-44). At the Last Supper, Jesus girded Himself with a towel, took a basin of water, and washed the disciples' feet. In so doing He portrayed His servant role.

One test for maturity is to become less self-centered. A maturing person has both an ability and willingness to see himself as one among many. Self-centered people almost always end up stuck with the self they are stuck on. A person wrapped up in himself makes a mighty small package. Self-centeredness is always self-defeating. It causes us to be disgusted with ourselves, cuts us off from our friends, and shrinks the boundaries of our world.

Service on the other hand opens up our lives to new adventures. One man explained it, "My life took on new meaning when I stopped selling houses and started selling homes." Service has the ring of genuineness. It makes us feel good deep down inside.

When relocating to Laurens, South Carolina, my wife and I moved into a house formerly owned by two sisters. The sisters because of age and declining health had found it necessary to leave their home of many years and to seek the needed care they then required. One sister entered the Laurens Health Care Center while the other went to live with a daughter in another state. My wife learned through neighbors the name of the sister in the nearby health care center. She also learned that the sisters had taken great pride in the way the yard was kept while they lived together. They grew many varieties of beautiful flowers. One day my wife cut some flowers from the yard which had been planted by the sisters and took a vase to the one in the health care center. I was amazed at the stir that act created when the word got around. A fellow church member stopped by the house to thank us for such a gracious act. The sister's minister thanked me profusely at the Rotary meeting. Actually, it was not my idea at all. It was the type of kindness my wife would do. But who gained the most by a simple act of kindness rendered in love? The sister's life was certainly enhanced. But our world grew too. The boundaries of our world were extended to encircle another person, and we were blessed thereby.

It was a red-letter day in my life when I discovered that the principles by which Christ lived work, really work, in life. Unself-centered living brings happiness, not only to the person involved, but to those who surround him. Statements have cropped up that testify to the above truth. Here are some of those statements:

You have not lived a perfect day, even though you have earned your money, if you have not done something for someone who can never repay you.

The troubles of the world could be eliminated if everyone would put himself in the other person's place.

The happiest people are those who discover that what they should be doing and what they are doing are the same things.

Our world is truly as big as our service and as small as our selfishness.

Our World . . . As Big As Our Faith — As Small As Our Doubt

"And what is faith? Faith gives substance to our hopes, and makes us certain of realities we do not see" (Hebrews 11:1, NEB). Faith is not so much a theological term to be debated as it is a way of living. Faith takes the realities of eternity and makes them real in the here and now, so that we live in the present as if those truths were already realized. Faith, therefore, colors how we think, feel, and act right now—so does doubt. And each day we have to decide which of the two ships we shall set sail on.

Faith is optimism in the face of difficult tasks. There is no better example of this quality than that found in Mother Teresa. When she was asked about the work of her religious community on behalf of the dying poor of Calcutta, she replied, "What we are doing is just a drop in the ocean. But if the drop was not in the ocean, I think the ocean would be less because of the missing drop."

Pessimism and doubt are usually born of inactivity. Those who are engaged in some beneficial undertaking are usually optimists, because they see the whole picture from the vantage point of their accomplishments. They are so busy lighting candles that they don't have time to curse the darkness.

Faith is venture, risk, and exploration with life. It remains true that whoever hoards his life ends up losing it. Where there is no venture, there is no discovery. The observation has been made that when Columbus set out on his journey across the sea, he didn't know where he was going; when he arrived, he didn't know where he was; and when he returned, he didn't know where he had been—but all the same he discovered America.

Rebecca Johnson, 23, decided to test her endurance by paddling a canoe down the Mississippi from Minnesota to the Gulf of Mexico— alone. Along the way she met plenty of people who predicted she would never make it.

"When I got to within 200 miles of New Orleans, people asked me where I was going and then they'd say, 'Lady, that's a long way.' I'd say, 'Not when you've already paddled 2,200 miles!' "[1]

Faith is companionship with God. I well remember the night it happened. Mildred, my wife, and I had returned from church on a Sunday evening. I was reading the daily Bible reading from our church literature. It was that portion of Scripture where Jesus sent His disciples, two by two, on a mission. They were not to take with them staves, nor scrip, neither bread nor money (Luke 9:3). They were to abide in the houses of those who would receive them. When they returned from their journey, Jesus asked them if they had lacked for anything. Their reply was, "Nothing" (Luke 22:35).

Right then and there it hit me. I had been feeling for awhile that God was calling me to be a minister. To me that call meant preparation. At that point preparation included at least college. But here I was, married, with house and furniture payments. College, from a financial point of view, was impossible. But there was that "Nothing" with which I had to deal. The disciples had lacked for nothing. God's voice broke through to me in that Scripture. He asked, "Why don't you believe that?" From that point on, there was no doubt what we would do. We would sell the house, launch out in faith, and travel the journey of life with God one step at a time.

Conclusion — Expanding Our World

How big is your world? How big do you want it to be? Each of us has a world with individual dimensions because each of us is different.

Every day we expand or shrink the size of our world by the attitudes we exhibit.

Professor Abraham Maslow used to challenge his students with questions like: "Which of you is gong to write the next novel?" and "Who is going to be a saint like Schweitzer?"

Confronted with such big ideas, the students would only blush and squirm. Then, the famed psychologist would assure them that he meant what he said.

"If not you, who will?" he would ask.[2]

May I ask again, how big do you want your world to be? It can be as big as your love and as small as your hate. It can be as big as your service and as small as your selfishness. It can be as big as your faith and as small as your doubt. You decide in every situation what the boundaries of your world will be. Always choose bigness.

1. *Christopher News Notes*, No. 229, 12 East 48 Street, New York, NY 10017.

2. Ibid.

10

When Religion Becomes Irreligious

Perversion of the good into the bad is a practice that can invade even the high and holy. Mere religion is not exempt from taking that which begins with a pure motive and lowering it to the base and selfish. The donning of religious garments and becoming deft in holy language are no guarantee that a religious act is free of hypocrisy or pretense. And, it may be added, to feel oneself to be totally devoid of the possibility of such low action is the foremost danger signal of falling victim to such a practice.

At what point, then, does religion become irreligious? When does one cross the boundary separating the good and holy from the bad and profane? What are some accurate guidelines by which we can measure the integrity of our actions?

Display or Innate Worth?

Religion becomes irreligious when acts of worship are practiced for display rather than for their innate worth (see Matthew 6:1). Jesus recited three instances in which the temptation to perform for display was especially present—almsgiving, prayer, and fasting.

Collections for the poor were frequent in the religious practices of Jesus' day, and there was plenty of opportunity for ostentatious giving. Therefore, Jesus gave the admonition that a trumpet not be blown—a figurative expression perhaps—to call attention to the act of giving and that the offering given was to be surrounded with secrecy — "let not thy let hand know what thy right hand doeth" (see Matthew 6:2-4).

The observation has been made that the insignificant, the empty, is usually the loud, and, as illustrated by the drum, is loud even because of its emptiness. When one has discovered the innate value of an act of worship such as almsgiving, the desire for display is minimized. Any student of the human personality knows that the loud and the boisterous indicate a lack of depth or else the loudness would not be necessary. The bully more often than not is a coward inside.

Public prayer is another act of worship where the tendency toward display is a lingering temptation (see Matthew 6:5). "Do not heap up empty phrases," Jesus warned (Matthew 6:7). Our prayers are rather to be childlike in simplicity. Children usually come to the point quickly with few disguises.

Fasting too must flee every inducement to spiritual pride (see Matthew 6:16-18). Mature Christians have no need to feel superior to other Christians. Their measure of greatness is not found in their being better than others but in their opportunities to serve others (see Luke 22:24-27).

Acts of worship, especially those that are public, should be done with dignity and grace. The reading of the Scripture, the singing of the hymns, the sermon, the prayers, the ushering, all should have the best in preparation. What we offer to God, whether private or public, must be of the highest caliber possible. But the acts of worship must be done well because of our desire to honor Him, not our desire for personal praise.

I once read that when we are praised for a given act, it makes it difficult to repeat that act with pure motive. The tendency is to think in terms of the praise received. I am not suggesting that praise be withheld. I rather am seeking to remind us of how thin the line is between performance for display and practicing for innate worth.

The late Chester Swor shares with us an event out of his own vast experience which illustrates how common it is to do good for the wrong reasons. He wrote, "We sat at the conclusion of a truly clever 'sweetheart banquet' in which the decorations, program, and food had vied with each other in their superlative excellence. Some people had worked hard, very hard, to make that banquet a glorious experience. The toastmaster thanked a round of people with appropriate eulogies, but he overlooked inadvertently the lady who had done most of the food preparation! Though the oversight was deplorable, it was surely not deliberate.

"The benediction had been pronounced, and almost everyone had departed. I stood in conversation with friends who were waiting for candlesticks to be gathered. Out of the kitchen came the overlooked lady. She was indignant almost to the point of volcanic explosion.

" 'They can just eat paper napkins up here from now on out, so far as I am concerned,' she declared. 'I came up here early this morning, worked my fingers to the bone nearly all day, and do you think that the toastmaster even so much as thanked me publicly? Indeed, he did not!' And she proceeded to whisk articles off the table with evident venom.

"As deplorable as was the toastmaster's oversight, more deplorable was this Christian woman's display of a selfish motivation for Christian service. It was evident that in her all-day toil in the kitchen, she had been imagining a scene at the end of the banquet: She would be called out of the kitchen; she would go, reluctantly, of course; and, as she stood in the limelight, the toastmaster would exhaust his supply of superlatives in eulogizing her; and, midst gales of applause, she would bow back to the kitchen in a blaze of glory! Though she had worked all day in a so-called Christian service, she had rendered no acceptable service. She was serving, not primarily for Jesus' sake, but because of her own selfish desires for praise and publicity."[1]

Prescribed Religious Regulations or Acts of Mercy?

Religion becomes irreligious when prescribed religious regulations supersede acts of mercy (see Mark 3:1-6). Mark's account of the man with the withered hand on the sabbath day is a prime example of Jesus' refusal to allow prescribed religious regulations to override the giving of mercy to one in need. Jesus was already quite at variance with the orthodox religious leaders of His day. For Him to be in the temple at all was to be in the danger zone. Surely some test case as to His approach to the law would appear, and it did. It came in the form of a man with a withered hand. Would Jesus heal him on the sabbath? Would He show total disregard for the law? The religious leaders would watch Him closely and see (v. 2).

If Jesus had been a cautious, prudent person, He would have conveniently arranged not to see the man; for He knew that to heal the man was asking for trouble. The law forbade work on the sabbath day. Medical attention could only be given if a life were in danger. This man's life was not in the least danger. Physically he would be no worse off if he were left until the following day. But for Jesus, this was a test case; and He met it fairly and squarely.

To the Pharisee, religion was ritual; it meant obeying certain rules and regulations. To Jesus religion was service. It was love of God and love of neighbor. To Jesus the most important consideration was not the correct performance of a ritual but the spontaneous answer to the cry of human need. And so, Jesus said to the man, "Stretch forth thine hand." Then and there He healed him.

When someone is hurting, we should not run to our religious rule book—that is if we have one—but to our first aid kit. Human need supersedes religious orthodoxy. One only has to consult the Scripture to see how Jesus again and again placed acts of mercy above prescribed religious regulation. The weightier matters of the law consisted of judgment, mercy, and faith (see Matthew 23:23). The entirety of the law could be summed up in love for God and love for one's neighbor. He defined neighbor not in terms of geographical location, or in terms of race, or in any other superficial designation, but in terms of acts of mercy—being a neighbor (see Luke 10:30-37).

Some of the harshest people whom I have encountered in my ministry have been religious people who place law above mercy. Their concept of the Christian faith seems to be to obey the rules, no matter the person's need. It isn't an unusual happening to find Christians with stones in hand ready to pounce on anyone who violates their prescribed code of religious conduct. It doesn't seem to matter that in enforcing the rule one tramples upon the weightier matter of mercy. Religion becomes irreligious when prescribed religious rules supersede acts of mercy.

Societal Values or Christian Values?

Religion becomes irreligious when societal values become equated with Christian values. What is it to be essentially Christian is a question with which we must wrestle again and again. Societal values tend to spill over into the Christian community and become equated with Christian values.

Christianity is an insurgent gospel. It often flatly contradicts the accepted order. It is a challenge flung into the teeth of standards that we often take for granted: "It shall not be so among you" (Matthew 20:26).

The desire for greatness and power are two areas with which Jesus dealt in indicating to us the revolutionary nature of His teaching. The world's idea of greatness and power is like a pyramid—with the great and powerful standing at the peak and with most other people scrambling to reach the next higher level where there are fewer equals and more subordinates. But Christ's idea of greatness and power is like an inverted pyramid where the nearer the top one reaches, the heavier the burden and more the servanthood (see Matthew 20:26-28).

The telltale questions that float around at our religious conventions are indicative of how much the standards of Satan have entered the precincts of the Divine. Introductory questions about family and place of lodging are quickly dispensed with in order to get to the "real issues"—What size is your church? What is its budget? How many are on staff? These are subtle questions because underneath the real questions are—How much greatness? How much power? Very seldom, if at all, do we ask the questions which indicate Christian values. What attitudes are basic in our lives? Are we ready to be last, if truly we can honor Christ? Do we practice self-sacrifice? Do we serve without acclaim?

Connely Chandler was a deacon in my first pastorate. He lived in an old Presbyterian manse surrounded by three acres of land. He never owned a car. He didn't like to lead in public prayer. He was not known beyond his own immediate community. And yet, when my mind wanders back to those people who touched my life with love and challenged me to serve, Connely Chandler stands at the top of the list. His motives were so pure; his service was rendered with no desire for acclaim; his deep caring sprang from an inner life fed from the river of God's eternal grace. His value system, though simple, was profound: love Christ and love your neighbor. Therein is greatness.

Societal standards may assess a person's greatness by the number of people whom he controls (power), "but it shall not be so among you." The world may judge a person by the job he holds, or the house in which he lives, or even by the car that he drives, "but it shall not be so among you." Societal values may lay acclaim to a person's titles, his degrees, his position, "but it shall not be so among you." He that is greatest among you is he who serves—a cup of water to the thirsty, a visit to the lonely, a word of love to the outcast, a tender touch to those beaten by life's hardships. These acts of love, and these alone, meet the value system which was taught by Christ. Societal values must not be allowed to infiltrate the Christian community and replace the revolutionary values of Christ.

Superiority or Genuineness?

Religion becomes irreligious when religious terminology or religious acts are used to indicate one's spiritual superiority over another rather than springing from a motivation of genuineness. True greatness does not have to parade itself. Genuineness does not gain its genuineness by demeaning someone else or by making comparison to someone else. The prayer of the Pharisee in the temple, "I am not as other men" (Luke 18:11), was ineffective because in God's measurements reality is more important than comparisons made. It would be hard to imagine an Albert Schweitzer or a Mother Teresa looking about and noting, "See how superior I am to others."

Dwight L. Moody was once passing a church when some young-sters came out. He stopped to inquire what they had been up to. "We have been inside praying," they replied. "See how our faces shine." The evangelist's quiet reply was, "Moses didn't know that his face was shining."

It is disturbing to observe the subtle ways we go about trying to prove our spiritual superiority to others. A minister once shared with me about a testimony given in his church by a lady who claimed God had miraculously healed her. Not once in her testimony did she mention the medication which he knew she was taking. Her pastor had no doubt about God's power to heal. He simply wondered how she could overlook so obvious a factor as medication being taken.

Very often certain words or catch phrases are thrown into our conversation because they have come to represent in the popular mind some sort of religious stance which rises above the common lot. These words or phrases when used with the proper intonation usually bring a chorus of amens. It is interesting to note, however, that the areas with which these words or phrases deal are not the simple acts of kindness by which Christ said we would be judged—water to the thirsty, food to the hungry, a visit to those who are sick or who are in prison. Those who seek to be superior to others usually avoid dealing in the concrete dimensions of life where talk can be evaluated by corresponding action.

When Paul spoke of the way of love in 1 Corinthians 13, he defined love in terms of concrete, measurable outcomes. Love is kind, is not rude, does not rejoice in wrong. All of these outcomes of love are non-bragging areas. Imagine someone seeking to prove himself more spiritual than someone else by stating how he had been less rude. The very desire to appear to be superior to others indicates a lack of genuineness and depth in our Christian faith.

Deep Religious Feelings or Exploited Emotions?

Religion becomes irreligious when deep religious feelings are exploited in order to attain some selfish goal. Religious feelings are perhaps as intense or even more intense than in any other area. This very fact makes exploitation an ever-present possibility. Those persons who choose to exploit emotions in order to gain power, prestige, or economic advantage find fertile soil in the religious community.

The trial and crucifixion of Jesus is a prime example of how deep religious feelings can be exploited to attain a given end. Matthew 15:11 reads, "But the chief priests stirred up the crowd to have him (Pilate) release for them Barabbas." There was much in Barabbas to win the vote over Jesus in the courtyard of Pilate, and the religious leaders knew it. So, they began their exploitation.

For one thing, Barabbas was a nationalist. He had a common-sense slogan which appealed directly to the emotions—"Judea for the Judeans." To many his intense patriotism had far more attraction than Jesus had, with all that talk about loving one's enemy.

Barabbas was also a man of violence. To him the ultimate goal justified the means. Life was clear-cut and straightforward. He provided an outlet whereby the masses did not have to deal with ambivalence. "Isn't there another side to the issue?" is an unthinkable question to those bent on destroying the imagined enemy. Get a club. Use muscle. You need not use your brain. Such a simple approach, with the added element of violence, seems so much more practical than the words of Jesus which advocated that we become peacemakers.

To Barabbas the source of evil also was external. The enemy was the hated Romans. Drive them from the land, and all would be well. It never occurred to him that external conflicts have their wellspring in the hearts of men. So this Jesus, who called for repentance, a change of heart, was far too complex and difficult for the people to fathom. Neither did He stand a chance in competing with the appeal to the people made by the religious leaders.

An immeasurable insight provided by the story of Jesus' crucifixion is the clear way it shows how Jesus was pushed to His death by motives which continuously find play in our own lives. We are capable and sometimes resort to the same sins active in the howling mob in the courtyard and at the foot of the cross. Patriotism, pride, lifeless tradition, prejudice all can be appealed to in order to stir up the crowds for our own evil purposes. The sin of emotional rabble-rousing is one the religious community knows well. It is a common and powerful force. It can and does lead to loss of a job, to unbridled cruelty, to murder, to war.

One story coming out of my own childhood was that of a father and daughter who graduated from high school at the same time. The unusual happening created quite a stir in our small town. It served as a conversation piece whenever people gathered.

Later in life the father, who was the source for so many positive emotions when he completed high school, committed an act which became the talk of our community. He murdered his wife of many years. Why would a person who appeared to be a gentle man commit such a crime? No one could say for sure.

There was, however, another part to the story of the father which I had heard told many times. When he was a child, his father had been accused of a crime. Early one morning, a masked mob appeared at the home place. The young child's father was dragged away and hanged. There was no trial. There was no jury—except the mob. I often wondered upon hearing of the father's murder of his wife how much effect the lynching of his own father had upon the sorry episode. Did those who became caught up in the hysteria of the mob play a part in a murder?

Many of the criticisms hurled at Jesus were intended to arouse negative emotional reactions from religious people that would serve as a power base to destroy Him. He is not Moses' friend—that is, His view of the Old Testament doesn't coincide with ours. He violates the sabbath—that is, people are more important to Him than rules. He eats with publicans and sinners—that is, He breaks our religious social codes. Whenever we allow ourselves to be driven into emotional stampedes by disguised religious chatter designed to accomplish certain evil ends, we commit the same sin as those who cried out, "Crucify Him." For we crucify anew our Christ in every fresh injustice which comes about when blind emotion begins to see red.

Conclusion

A part of redemption includes saving us from our base selves. It cuts through the outward act to discern the motivation underlying the act. It seeks to correlate the heart with the hands and feet. Redemption's goal is to make us genuine. Christ referred to it as wholeness.

No one of us is immune to taking holy things and using them for evil purposes. Satan's greatest victories are not won on pagan battle-fields but amid those people who claim kingdom membership. To keep the good undiluted by the bad is our strongest challenge. Not to allow the religious to become irreligious must be our constant theme.

1. Chester E. Swor, *Very Truly Yours* (Nashville: Broadman Press, 1954), 141-42.

11

Are You Ready to Forgive?

No theme prevails in the New Testament like that of forgiveness, except perhaps love. The close correlation between the themes of forgiveness and love is seen in Ephesians 4:32: "Be kind and compassionate to one another, forgiving each other, just as in Christ God forgave you."

Forgiveness offered or received calls for understanding the process of timing. When forgiveness is prematurely offered or received, it has the note of unreality. People often have to work through their hurt to arrive at the point of forgiveness. Genuineness in forgiveness must take into account the factor of readiness — thus, the question which heads this chapter: "Are You READY to Forgive?"

There are three prevailing assumptions about forgiveness that need to be reevaluated. Let me briefly mention the three areas, and then return later in the chapter to a more detailed explanation.

First, we have assumed that if people understood they should forgive, they automatically would know how to forgive. So little attention has been given to the how. The result is that many good people who believe strongly that to forgive is a basic tenet of the Christian faith go on hating and holding deep-seated grudges. They are convicted they should forgive, but the how is missing.

Second, we have assumed that forgiveness is primarily an instantaneous act, and, because of that premise, little attention has been given to forgiveness as a process. As stated earlier in this book, there is a mind-set inclined to see more of the miraculous in that which happens momentarily than in that which occurs over time. It is almost as if forgiveness can be offered or received with virtually no consideration given to what preceded the act itself, or to the implications of what is to follow. Almost all the emphasis is centered on the moment of decision, that time when the process leaps into the open.

Third, we have assumed that forgiveness is an individual act with little or no communal ramifications. The truth is that when a person would step outside prevailing traditions of ingrained hatreds held by family or clan members—even to suggest that forgiveness of the enemy might be a solution—is to place oneself in the danger zone. Group hatreds do not surrender tamely to any violator of conventional practices.

Now, let's return to the three assumptions about forgiveness mentioned earlier and deal with each one in more detail. At this point I also need to acknowledge my indebtedness to various sources provided on the subject under consideration,and especially to the *Christopher News Notes* (No. 242) for its profound and practical exploration on the how of forgiveness. Intertwined in the material to follow will be not only the writer's personal insight, but the accumulation of what he has gathered through the years. The particular origin of a given understanding may long have been forgotten, but not the understanding itself.

First, we must give more attention to the *how* of forgiveness, not merely the *what*. There are many persons who sincerely want to forgive, but who need help in how to go about it. There are no magic formulas here, no easy solutions, only a few suggestions.

Spend Time with Christ

Exposure to models is one of the most dynamic forces in learning. Example is the greatest teacher. Christian truth is transmitted relationally rather than propositionally. Truth in action is undeniably effective. It is out of associations that permanent change takes place.

In addition to the two most-often-mentioned ways of spending time with Christ—namely Bible study and prayer—add one other suggestion. Open your mind and heart to exploration with Christ as companion and guide. Let your thoughts soar. Remove restrictive boundaries. Be ready to travel new paths. Be unafraid to feel deeply. Identify your feeling responses to given situations. Keep in touch with who you are, but maintain a ready willingness to change with the promptings of the Spirit.

Imagine what would happen if a bigot with his pattern of prejudicial thinking and feeling began walking the trail of life with Christ at his side. Would he continue to be rude? Love is not rude. Would he still make his slurring remarks? God is no respecter of persons. Would he treat others with disdain? Christ came to call all people to repentance with no one excluded. It is impossible to rub shoulders on a day-to-day basis with the Great Forgiver without learning how to forgive. His example will teach us.

Remove the Halo

Christians with halos seldom ask for or extend forgiveness. Why not? Because they are always dealing from a superior to inferior position. They, like the Pharisee praying in the temple, are not like other men. When we deal from the position of equality, forgiveness becomes more of a possibility.

Self-righteous individuals usually are more interested in proving that they are right than in healing relationships. Once we jump over the hump of placing blame, or needing always to be right, a firm step has been taken in the direction of forgiveness.

Occasionally in a worship service I will ask the people to lift their hands in the manner that they would be used in removing a halo from one's head. Through this symbolic act, enforcement is given to the truth that halos block vital relationships. Only with their removal are we ready to engage in serious confession of our sins.

Look squarely at the injury you have done or that has been done to you. Acknowledge any feelings of guilt or resentment. Be totally honest here, for religious people in particular often refuse to admit feelings they think they ought not to have.

When the writer was at the First Baptist Church of Charlotte, phone calls asking for directions to the church were frequent. One of the first points to be established when giving directions is where the person is at the time. It is impossible to give directions without that information. The same is true with forgiveness. In order to forgive or be forgiven, we need to know what the particular is. We need to know where we are with our feelings.

We cannot circumvent feelings in forgiveness—we have to go through them. That is why it is necessary to comprehend what our true feelings are. Pushing them down or denying their existence only makes the issue worse.

Without forgiveness these feelings will harden and deepen. So, we have to decide whether or not we want to live that way for the remainder of our lives.

Become Decisive

Learn to exercise the will. Forgiveness eventually becomes a choice. As we move in the direction of maturity, the will more and more rides herd over the feelings. Feelings are readily acknowledged, but they do not control altogether our choices.

When the will is exercised in positive choice, the feelings tend to fall in line. It may take them awhile to get there, but get there they will. Each action we take to carry out the decision we have made works to alter our feelings in keeping with the decision.

One night when driving from Elon College, North Carolina, to Charlotte, I experienced the culmination of an adjustment period wherein my feelings had finally caught up with my will. My wife and I had made the decision to leave the First Baptist Church of Elon College, where we had served for 21 years, to go to a staff position at the First Baptist Church of Charlotte. Some six months had elapsed since that decision had been made, but there were still strong emotional ties to our former residence. So, driving alone at night, somewhere on the road from Elon College to Charlotte, it suddenly hit me that for the first time I was going home emotionally. My feelings had finally caught up with a decision I had been living out for six months.

That experience is descriptive of what happens when we decide to offer or accept forgiveness. It may require the feelings some time to fall into line. We begin the process by making a decision, and then, without rushing or over-delaying, we wait for the moment when wholeness arrives, that time when will, feelings, and action are on the same wavelength.

Do Something

Affirming a decision by immediate action strengthens the resolve. Zacchaeus announced publicly and in specific terms, immediately after his encounter with Jesus, what he was going to do (Luke 19:8). Stating his intention openly brought other people in on his resolve. They could now become monitors of his progress.

Recently I joined a group in our Discipleship Training program entitled "First Place." At our initial meeting each person announced to the whole group what his intended weight loss was. The group then became encouragers, as well as monitors, as we moved toward our stated goal. Sharing our intention with others works in that we are no longer a lone wolf battling the elements alone, but it becomes a corporate endeavor in which others participate in the race with us.

Specific goals have more punch than general goals. No goal becomes dynamic until it becomes specific. My stated weight loss goal in First Place therefore was 30 pounds, not "I need to lose some weight."

Monitoring began immediately in that our first action at each group meeting was to weigh in. Records were kept of our progress toward our goal. In fact, we recorded our weight gain or loss on a sheet for all to see. There was a sense of group pride as individual members experienced success.

Forgiveness, either granted or received, needs to be followed immediately with some overt act. It can be as simple as a touch on the shoulder or as radical as the denunciation of a destructive way of life.

Think of forgiveness as the greatest gift you can give or receive. Forgiveness cannot be earned or forced. It is a gift to be offered freely or received thankfully.

But think what forgiveness accomplishes. It repairs the broken fences. It removes the tense atmosphere. It allows us to talk to one another, to express affection, to enjoy being together. No greater gift can be given or received.

Each one of us has the opportunity to give or receive such a gift almost daily. It may be as common as giving or accepting an apology, or it may be as profound as having a heavy load of guilt removed.

Practice one-way forgiveness when two-way forgiveness is impossible. The response to our desire to forgive may be a withholding of forgiveness by the other party involved. At such a time, we can give forgiveness silently in the heart.

Learning to work on the factors over which we have some control, rather than majoring on matters over which we have little control, is one of the arts of living. We can waste scads of energy needlessly when we center our attention on the other person's response rather than our response. Furthermore, majoring on the other person's reaction can become, and is often used as, a scapegoat whereby we justify a return to the state of animosity. Sometimes the only door open to us is to be decisive about what we will do about a given estrangement. The one latch we can control is on our side of the door.

Consider the possibility that some injuries are unintentional or even unavoidable. Not every hurt should be taken as a deliberate affront. We need to avoid the habit of always taking things personally.

Certain questions asked about the other party involved may improve our understanding of the situation.

What temperament is the norm for this person? Were there pressures being felt that precipitated a given reaction? What would I have done under similar circumstances? Once we make an attempt to try to understand where the other person is coming from, forgiveness becomes easier, even desired.

Practice Total Forgiveness

Forgiveness is total or it is nothing. It is impossible to forgive half a wrong. Conditional forgiveness has an empty ring. When we attach an "if" or a "but" to forgiveness, we undercut the process.

Total forgiveness doesn't mean, however, that certain guidelines regarding future action are ignored. A family member who has used the credit card unwisely needs to know that monitoring will occur until the trust level is reestablished. The philandering husband or wife should be made aware that unexplained late-night activities will not be tolerated, but constant reminders or withheld gratuities indicate partial forgiveness, and such will not work. Strong-arm tactics have a way of blowing up on us.

Build a Life-style of Forgiving

A life-style is established by practicing certain responses until they become the norm. We do not have to force ourselves to be a given way—we simply are. There is harmony between what we are on the inside and our outward expression. A healthy pattern has been formed.

Forgiveness needs to become a life habit. It should not be an issue over which we debate endlessly. When a broken relationship occurs, we move automatically in the direction of resolving the conflict. There is unrest in our inner being until the troubled waters have become calm.

These suggestions on the "how" of forgiveness listed previously are given to aid the many people who sincerely want to forgive, but have struggled with the how. The ultimate goal intended is the practical application of the Christian faith in everyday life experiences, with the result being the expansion of our world.

Now let's return briefly to the other two assumptions about forgiveness which need to be reevaluated—namely, that we have dealt with forgiveness primarily as an instantaneous act, and have given little attention to forgiveness as a process, and that forgiveness is an individual act with little or no communal implications.

Forgiveness as a Process

Our inclination in forgiveness is to focus on the point of decision, that time when exposure takes place, and to give little attention to what preceded the decision, or to the implications of what is to follow the decision. Genuine, meaningful decision is preceded by certain preparations, and is followed by positive actions inherent in the decision;

otherwise "readiness" to forgive is violated. An issuance of forgiveness prior to the time when we have worked through the feelings connected with the problem area carries a note of unreality. We need to recognize where we are along the continuum so the decision will not be rushed or delayed. There are times when honesty would have us confess, "We are not ready yet to forgive. We are working in that direction. When the time is ripe, the decision will be made, but not now."

To seek proper timing in our desire to forgive should not carry with it the factor of guilt. Our goal is genuineness. So to withhold the offer to forgive until we can do so with our whole being is the proper and healthy approach.

Viewing forgiveness as a process means giving consideration to the implications that follow the overt act. What changes in life-style are implied in the decision? What behavioral alterations are needed?

Quite often we do not know the end from the beginning. As a result we have to learn along the way how to readjust. Certain feelings may arise that we didn't anticipate. These feelings must be dealt with. Suppose, for example, the original estrangement was the result of sexual indiscretion. We cannot know what feelings will arise when we engage for the first time in the conjugal act. Sometimes the movement toward true union is blocked until we can sort out our feelings and work through them.

The attention given here to forgiveness as a process is not an attempt to undermine the importance of the decisive moment, or to de-emphasize the nature of the miraculous involved. It is an effort to call to our attention the need for genuineness, and, that for genuineness to occur we must consider what precedes the decision, and what follows it.

Forgiveness in Community

The third assumption about forgiveness that we need to reconsider is that forgiveness is an individual act with practically no communal ramifications or consequences. The approach has been that if one wants to forgive, it is his business and his business alone. But is that how it works? No. When an individual chooses a course of action that violates traditional hatreds of family or clan, that choice is immediately challenged. The reason for the defiance is that when one member acts out of keeping with the common practices of the group, it sends a disturbing message to the other members. Here is one who is breaking the established pattern. Does that mean we need to change? How many of the group will be influenced by this violator of the prevailing code?

Ripples appear on the water anytime that fixed behavior is breached. The reaction by the group may be as slight as a disagreeable facial expression, or as intense as murder of the transgressor. The intensity of the opposition to Jesus, for example, was in direct proportion to the repercussions he was causing amid the religious groups of that day. His every action elicited a reaction. So challenging was Jesus' behavior to the set patterns deemed appropriate that the religious leaders concluded that the only way to settle the matter was to kill Him!

A person's individual choices, then, are never isolated from the family or clan of which he is a member. So, to forgive when that forgiveness runs contrary to what the group wants is to truly place oneself in the danger zone.

In conclusion, let me affirm that there are two important questions in the Christian community, and the answers to those questions are vastly different.

The first question has to do with whether or not forgiveness is a basic tenet of the Christian faith. The answer to that question is a resounding "Yes!"

The second question, which deals with whether or not we are ready to forgive, is one to which we must give more attention, because readiness determines genuineness, and genuineness determines value. Unless we understand how to apply a profound truth, the truth itself can become a burden instead of a relief.

Majoring on what we are to do, to the neglect of how we are to do it, is no longer an acceptable course of action. Therefore, my goal for this chapter is to give help to those persons who believe deeply in forgiveness, but who sometimes struggle in their application of it. If the insights shared somehow help in the expansion of your world through the rightful application of forgiveness to specific issues, then my joy will be complete.

12

Living Creatively Amid Conformity
Mark 2:21-22; 1 Peter 1:13;
1 Corinthians 12:4-7

Painter Georgia O'Keeffe was the subject of a television special honoring her 90th birthday. In this portrait of the artist, Ms. O'Keeffe remembered that she had tried in her youth to find a mentor who could teach her how to paint landscapes. Finally she stopped trying.

"They could tell me how they painted their landscapes," she said, "but they couldn't tell me how to paint mine."

One of the supreme challenges of life is how to live creatively amid the pressures to conform—to maintain one's own uniqueness when the call of the hour is to fit in.

Each person has something different to offer. "There is a variety of gifts but always the same Spirit; there are all sorts of service to be done, but always to the same Lord; working in all sorts of different ways in different people, it is the same God working in all of them" (1 Corinthians 12:4-7). Perhaps one of our major sins is that we develop one mold, and then go all out to make everyone adapt.

The Creative Christ

Jesus is a prime example of one who carved out His own niche, who refused to settle for the status quo. Had He conformed He could have become an accepted member of any one of many religious groups of His day. But He didn't.

Mark 2 records three violations by Jesus of the accepted religious code.

The first break with tradition was association with the wrong crowd (vv. 13-17). He ate with tax collectors and sinners. "Pious" people never seem to understand that "association with" doesn't always mean "agreement with." Neither do they understand that "association with"

87

is our most potent tool for helping. Isolation from the common lot may look good on the religious chart, but it is ineffective in effecting change.

A second violation of the religious code was the neglect of fasting (vv. 18-20). Again, pious persons tend to place emphasis on correct and regular observances rather than timing and meaning. It was not that Jesus was against fasting; it was that the mood of the occasion called for another tone.

A third offense was the failure to observe sabbath regulations (vv. 23-28). To the super pious ones, religious guidelines tower over human need. They choose to hem in the value even of the sabbath by placing emphasis on restrictions rather than purpose and design.

Jesus' critics were not asking Him to stop being religious but to start being religious their way. An intriguing aspect of the religious pilgrimage is that patterns develop which, at first, had purpose and meaning, but later on are allowed to become restrictive when new insight and expanded understanding are forthcoming. The old is not always good simply because it is old, no more than the new is always good just because it is new. When to let go of that which would impede the meaningful present, and to latch onto the creative moment, is wisdom indeed.

Jesus' warning that we cannot take the new and dynamic and cram it into old restrictive patterns is a difficult lesson to learn (vv. 21-22). We want to hold onto old forms long after their usefulness is gone. Sometimes the only way to move into the new is to discard the old. New cloth sewn on old garments neither works nor looks good. New, expanding wine, when poured into old wineskins that have lost their elasticity, causes them to burst.

Creativity Versus Conformity

How, then, does one live creatively amid the pressures to conform? How does a person affirm his own uniqueness when the forces about him insist that he fit in?

First Peter 1:13 encourages us to be our own person, to live creatively. Various renderings of the verse emphasize its call for originality.

"Free your minds, then, of encumbrances."

"Roll up your sleeves mentally."

"Go in for some hard thought."

"Tear down the fences that would hem you in mentally."

"Wherefore gird up the loins of your mind."

New ideas and new approaches are all about us. Creativity is a matter of opening ourselves to possibilities.

In the 1700s landowner Jonas Hanway refused to accept the fact that he had to get wet when it rained. Having seen a tent-like contraption used in the Orient as protection against the sun, he adapted it for rain. The umbrella was born.

Stymied when volunteers failed to keep their commitments to finish painting the church, the maintenance committee chairperson divided the surface into equal parts. On each section, in large, bold letters, he painted the name of a remiss volunteer. The job was soon done.

A word that is being widely used at the present is "paradigm." It has to do with model or pattern. More specifically, its present usage refers to the pattern or model through which we look at things, events, or people. The trend is to develop a given paradigm that becomes standardized, and thereafter to view everything through that one pattern, thereby stifling creativity. By taking a fresh look and seeing matters differently, we can make all kinds of discoveries. We can replace old perceptions with new ones. We can combine old ideas in new ways and bring into being something which didn't exist before. How open are you?

One of my roles for many years has been the training of adult Sunday School leaders in the "how" of teaching. Sensing that teachers had not picked up on the relation between aims and methods, the search was on for a new way to illustrate the point. The quest was shared with a member of the church where I was pastor, along with a description of the object needed for the illustration. "Let me build you something out of plastic," he suggested.

The result was a square piece of clear plastic, made up of several pieces, put together with bolts and screws, which takes six different tools to take it apart, in order to extricate a small, steel ball in the very center. The procedure is to show the teachers the square piece of plastic which is named a "gizmo," and to explain that the aim is to remove the steel ball from the center. Then, while the teachers watch, each tool is used at its needed time in removing the pieces of plastic in order to reach the steel ball. When the process is completed, the point is made that methods are like tools—they help us accomplish aims. When we know what tools are available, develop skills in how to use them, and have the experience to know when a given tool is needed, our effectiveness as teachers will be greatly increased.

Four high school boys, afflicted with spring fever, skipped morning classes. After lunch, they reported to the teacher that the car had a flat tire on the way to school.

Much to their relief, she just smiled and said, "Well, you missed a test this morning, so take seats apart from one another and get out your notebooks."

Still smiling, she waited for them to settle down. Then she said, "First question: which tire was flat?"

So, creativity isn't a way of life reserved only for those people with exceptional talent. It means taking what we see and know and putting it together in a new way that makes sense and works.

Again, creative people are those who refuse to be hemmed in by things as they are, who believe there is more to truth than they possess at the moment, and who are willing to take the risks involved in walking new paths.

There are three distinct approaches used to hem in new understanding and make it fit things as they are. For one thing we can squeeze it to death. When we begin to see the enormity of a given truth, our reaction may be, "Wait a minute, this is too big to handle. If we carry out this new insight to its full implication, fundamental change will be necessary." So we begin to back up, to rationalize, to reduce. After all, we don't want to appear to be eccentric. Being off is not a course we find comfortable. Therefore, let us smooth off the rough edges so they don't grate against established patterns. Squeezing it a little bit won't hurt. But in squeezing it, we kill it.

Another approach used to hem in new truth is to trim it down to size. Instead of making the doorway bigger to accommodate the expanded concept, we simply trim down the concept to fit the doorway. After all, established patterns are not to be violated, cultural practices must be adhered to, and theological tenets are not to be disturbed.

A third approach used to hem in new insight is to throw the most vital away and keep only those elements that are least obtrusive. The goal here is to water down, to weaken, to discard, until it is no longer troubling. Hem it in, even if it means robbing it of its uniqueness.

One religious educator has graphically described the process whereby we begin to be hemmed in by worn concepts and set thinking patterns. He muses that as we begin life it is like a house with many open doors and windows. Things can easily get in and out. Then, slowly, almost imperceptibly, we begin to close the doors and windows, restricting, and finally forbidding, either entry or departure. Our house is built. New rooms are not to be added or old ones disturbed or taken away. We are comfortable with our house as it is. We stand ready to defend it at all costs. Disquieting questions about our house are either ignored or given pat answers in keeping with our limited quarters, for easy answers are always available when we have lived in the same house for many years.

Creative people believe that there is more to truth than they possess at the moment. Their understanding at best is partial. Like Paul they now see in part. Eternity alone will allow for full fruition.

Having such a perspective allows for growth. Since we know that our understanding is only partial, we are open to additional insight. The windows and doors to the houses of our lives are kept open, allowing for ready entry or quick exit. The rooms are altered to meet present need. Furnishings are rearranged so the expanded concepts feel at home.

One of the dire tragedies of life is that we often bring closure to a given truth long before we have the knowledge or experience for that truth to expand. Smallness of vision is the result. Dogmatism reigns, because nailing down a belief too early usually develops a know-it-all attitude. A recognition that our truth is partial, on the other hand, lends itself to greater tolerance and a willingness to join others in the search for wider understanding.

Maintaining such openness is not a sign of weakness but of strength. Retaining the capacity to change is a mark of courage. Covering virgin territory calls for bravery. But without exploration there is no discovery. Creative people, therefore, are willing to take the risks involved in walking new paths—and there are risks. Early on, those persons who have everything nailed down, who have developed structured behavior patterns, will begin to label you, because your every existence becomes a threat to them. The label "friend of sinners" given to Jesus by the Pharisees is a prime example of what happens when an individual dares to violate the prevailing religious code. Labels are usually chosen on the basis of the amount of emotional response they engender. Mob psychology, grounded in emotion, remains one of the most effective ways to destroy an individual or group. Those persons, bent on rendering ineffective anyone who differs, have learned well how to appeal to base emotions in their attack. One good definition for labels is that they are devices used by talkative people to save them the trouble of thinking.

Another risk is: we may discover that our former house no longer fits our beliefs. Even our wardrobe may have to be changed. One man noted that his tailor was the wisest man he knew, because every time he visited him, new measurements were taken perchance the old ones proved to be out of date. Creative people welcome positive change. It becomes a life-style for them. They trust their abilities to make choices, because they have entrusted those abilities to Christ.

When I was on staff at the First Baptist Church of Charlotte, fellow church members kept encouraging me to publish those prayers used in the regular worship services. One of those prayers entitled, "Thank You, Lord," and found in the book, *Expanding the Mind and Heart Through Prayer*, expresses my deep appreciation for what God has done in my life thus far, and a serene confidence in what He will do in the future.

Thank you, Lord

Thank you, Lord, for taking me where I was and helping me to become what I am.

Bashful, struggling to know, reaching out for love, all these were mine.

Then You found me, and gave me a purpose that overcame them all.

Today all boredom is gone.

My goals for life far supersede the time left in years.

Eternity alone will allow for full fruition.

Continue, O God, to touch my life in new and dynamic ways.

In Christ's name, Amen.

Again, creative people develop a broad knowledge base from which to proceed. The broader the knowledge base, the wider the possibility for creativity.

Being creative, then, is not sitting around waiting for "it" to happen. It involves learning the fundamentals. Painters must know how to paint. Poets need to know poetry. Teachers are to know how people learn. Mastering the basics in whatever area we are exploring enhances the potential for creativity.

Once I was sitting beside an assistant basketball coach as he watched the team go through certain drills. Suddenly he shouted at one of the players, "Why did you bounce the ball? You didn't go anywhere." Then and there I learned one fundamental in playing basketball. The only reason for bouncing the ball is that you are going somewhere. To bounce the ball when you have no intention of moving increases the possibility of needless errors. You can double dribble. The chances of the ball being stolen increase. Passing the ball to an open player becomes less likely. Knowing this fundamental about basketball allows the player to play the game on a higher, more creative level.

Expanding the knowledge base in whatever endeavor we undertake is a way of staying alive, energetic, even happy. When we know how to do, the doing becomes a thrill. Improvement becomes a constant goal. Creativity governs.

Another characteristic of creative people is that they avoid the roadblocks that stifle innovation. The *Christopher News Notes* in its pamphlet on the subject "Creativity," gave a list of those attitudes and mental habits that suppress creativity. They are as follow:

1. Excessive need for order. This encourages inflexible thinking and discourages originality.

2. Reluctance to play—with things, ideals, words, people. Individuals who are afraid of "looking silly" rarely innovate.

3. Resource myopia. Society values realism, i.e., seeing things as they are, whereas innovation requires seeing things as they might be.

4. Reluctance to risk. Innovation depends on a willingness to stick one's neck out.

5. Reluctance to exert influence. Fear of seeming "pushy" result in acceptance of the established way of doing things, even when there is a better way.

6. Overcertainty. The "disease of specialists"—those who are experts or think they are—closes the mind to new approaches.

Also listed in that same pamphlet are those traits in whose presence creativity thrives.

Awareness. We are most deeply aware, say psychologists, in the areas in which we are most intensely committed.

Curiosity. Searching for the "how" and "why" of things broadens our perspective. It nurtures our ability to judge.

Openness to new ideas. Inventor Thomas Alva Edison once said: "I'll try anything. I'll even try Limburger cheese!" The more we can keep the door open for a flow of ideas, the better the chance of usable solutions.

Patience with being unsettled. In the process of letting go of old answers and comfortable patterns there is anxiety. It is akin to the chemical process of fermentation which brings into being a new substance.

Sense of humor. Humor contains the same opposing elements found in most definitions of creative behavior: playfulness and seriousness, originality and reality, nonsense and purpose, the irrational and the rational.

Let me add four other traits to those given immediately above:

Maintain a healthy sense of dissatisfaction. A key word in the statement is "healthy." A healthy dissatisfaction maintains pride in one's own accomplishments while, at the same time, knowing that improvements can be made. The desire to do it better is a constant, but that desire is not allowed to rob the moment of meaning.

Develop wide associations. New ideas are seldom singularly achieved. They spring from an environment of creativity. So, stay in touch with creative people. Learn to talk to the wrong people. Usually talking to the right people means talking to individuals like ourselves, persons who will reverberate what we are already thinking.

Avoid labeling. Once we give ourselves a label, the label tends to take precedence over truth. Living in accord with the label becomes a must. Every thought or action that doesn't fit the tag is readily discarded irrespective of its value.

Develop a style that is uninhibited but not undisciplined. Being uninhibited does not mean being out of control. Worthwhile creativity must run the gauntlet of stern evaluation. It is not just growing in any direction. To the follower of Christ it means moving in the direction of God's truth arrived at on the basis of a disciplined mind and heart.

Again, creative people cooperate with the way their minds are made in order to be inventive. Years ago I came across a simple formula about how the mind works, which has been employed ever since in meeting the multiple demands of my profession. The thesis of the formula is that God made our minds a given way, and when we understand how our minds work, and cooperate with the process, we will be able to do more things and do them better. The formula is described by the use of three words.

Preparation—When given a task to perform or an assignment to complete, preparation refers to the conscious amount of time given. Preparation is the allotted time; it is scheduled time.

Creativity is not a lazy person's tool. We can't sit back and wait for it to happen. Dedicated work generates the atmosphere in which it can occur.

Incubation—My father would often say when a difficult decision was to be made, "Let me sleep on it." He probably never heard the word incubation, but he was practicing what it infers. He had learned from experience that the mind needs to be given time to work, and that it is working even when we are not aware of it. From the moment we undertake a task or assignment our minds are busy at work, and continue to work, both when we are aware and when we are not, until the job is completed.

Beginning early in order to give ample time for the mind to work is a necessary element in incubation. Creativity cannot be hurried. The mind does not produce its jewels when pressured by time limitation.

Illumination—Insight begins to come. Facets of truth hitherto unseen fill the mind. It's almost as if a flood of new understanding rushes over one. Concepts expand beyond imagination.

At this point the process described above is not a one, two, three happening. Further periods of preparation, followed by intermittent time for incubation, culminating in additional insight, is now the arrangement. Our minds are made to work like this. When we cooperate, our output will increase in quality and volume.

Finally, let it be said, living creatively is being ready for almost anything. When we join God in the adventure of life, we need not be surprised at whatever happens. God comes into our lives, not to destroy our individuality, but to affirm it. Even salvation itself, at least in part, is being rescued from the forces of conformity to become who we were intended to be. Sin is that ever-present temptation to settle for less than what Christ wants us to become. The greatest tragedy in life is that creativity can be strangled at birth. Carving out one's niche can be sacrificed in the face of hard-nosed practicality.

To be converted is to become like a child again, to know the thrill of life, to explore one's surroundings, to try the new and different. The child does not paint within the lines unless he is told he must. The roads he travels aren't all on the map until he is informed that there are no roads except those on the map.

Our challenge is not to let the forces of conformity override the will to explore, to maintain our uniqueness at all cost, to join hands with God as we walk together the high road of life.

Lay me on an anvil, O God.
Beat me and Hammer me
into a crowbar
Let me pry loose old walls.

Graphics by Byron Brown, Laurens First Baptist Church, Laurens, South Carolina.

Carl Sandburg, <u>Prayers of Steel</u>, cited in John Bartlett, <u>Familiar Quotations</u>, 13th edition, Boston; Little, Brown, copyright 1955, page 899.